Logic and Other Nonsense

✜

Logic and Other Nonsense

THE CASE OF ANSELM

AND HIS GOD

✤

ERMANNO BENCIVENGA

PRINCETON UNIVERSITY PRESS

PRINCETON, NEW JERSEY

Library of Congress Cataloging-in-Publication Data
Bencivenga, Ermanno, 1950–
Logic and other nonsense : the case of Anselm and his God /
Ermanno Bencivenga.
p.   cm.
Includes bibliographical references and index.
ISBN 0-691-07427-5
1. Anselm, Saint, Archbishop of Canterbury, 1033–1109.
2. Logic, Medieval.   3. God—Proof, Ontological.   I. Title.
B765.A84B46   1993
189'.4—dc20   93-18278
Excerpts from *Murder in the Cathedral* by T. S. Eliot,
copyright 1935 by Harcourt Brace Jovanovich, Inc., and
renewed 1963 by T. S. Eliot,
reprinted by permission of the publisher

This book has been composed in Bembo

Princeton University Press books are
printed on acid-free paper and meet the guidelines
for permanence and durability of the Committee
on Production Guidelines for Book Longevity
of the Council on Library Resources

Printed in the United States of America

1   3   5   7   9   10   8   6   4   2

TO ADA, MY MOTHER

✣

✢ Contents ✢

✣ *Preface* ✣

 Τ ΗΕ world happened, and everything else too, and it was all sort of déjà vu. I had no new clothes to put on, though lots of new lint. I had, I had . . . But that was then.

The day is shockingly bright now. Things have colors I didn't know existed. I noticed I have eyes.

And if this is not enough of a prayer, I wouldn't know what is.

Irvine, September 1992

✢ *Note on Texts* ✢

M<small>OST</small> Anselm quotes are from the *Opera omnia,* edited by F. Schmitt (Stuttgart-Bad Cannstatt: Friedrich Frommann Verlag, 1968). In each such quote, the roman numeral indicates the volume, and the arabic numeral the page. I have also used the *Memorials of St. Anselm* (abbreviated Me), edited by R. Southern and F. Schmitt (London: British Academy, 1969), the *Vita Sancti Anselmi* (abbreviated *Vita*) by Eadmer, edited by R. Southern (London: Thomas Nelson and Sons, 1962), and the *Historia novorum in Anglia* (abbreviated *Historia*) by Eadmer, edited by M. Rule (Wiesbaden: Kraus Reprint, 1965). All translations are mine. When applicable, I have supplied page references to J. Hopkins and H. Richardson's edition of the treatises (Toronto and New York: The Edwin Mellen Press, 1974–76); to W. Fröhlich's partial edition of the letters (Kalamazoo: Cistercian Publications, 1990 [abbreviated E]); to B. Ward's edition of the prayers and meditations (Harmondsworth: Penguin, 1973 [abbreviated O]); or to G. Bosanquet's edition of Eadmer's *Historia* (Philadelphia: Dufour, 1965 [abbreviated N]). In the references to Hopkins and Richardson's edition of the treatises, I have used the following abbreviations:

A = *Epistola de sacrificio azimi et fermentati*
C = *De concordia praescientiae et praedestinationis et gratiae dei cum libero arbitrio*
D = *De casu diaboli*
F = Philosophical fragments
G = *De grammatico*
H = *Cur deus homo*
I = *Epistola de incarnatione verbi*
L = *De libertate arbitrii*
M = *Monologion*
P = *Proslogion* (including the exchange with Gaunilo)
R = *Meditatio redemptionis humanae*
S = *De processione spiritus sancti*
Sa = *Epistola de sacramentis ecclesiae*
Ve = *De veritate*
Vi = *De conceptu virginali et de originali peccato*

Thus a typical reference would be I 24 M18, to be read: page 24 of volume I of Schmitt's edition, corresponding to page 18 of Hopkins and Richardson's edition of the *Monologion*.

The mottoes for the four chapters are from T. S. Eliot's *Murder in the Cathedral*. For references other than those above, see the Bibliography at the end.

Logic and Other Nonsense

✣

CHAPTER 1

The Program

We do not wish anything to happen.
Seven years we have lived quietly,
Succeeded in avoiding notice,
Living and partly living.

TRANSCENDENTAL CONCERNS

IN THE *Proslogion,* Anselm proves the existence and attributes of God. Why? What is the point of this operation? Right off, one could think of a couple of different ends he might have had in mind. One is to resolve his own doubts. I may not be sure that, say, neutrinos exist, hence it may be useful for me to go over the basic arguments for their existence. I may even be able to cook up some of my own. If and when that happens to my satisfaction, I will be convinced of (the truth of) something that before this operation was at best a conjecture: I will *know* (or think I do), whereas before I didn't.

But this is not what Anselm has in mind, it could not be. He begins his tour de force with an extended invocation to God; that prayer, in fact, constitutes the longest of the twenty-six chapters of the work. In the prayer, Anselm asks God to enlighten him, to appear to him, to offer to him that single, simple argument for His existence that he says in the proem he is looking for. And how can you address somebody if you don't know they are there? How can you summon their help if they might turn out to be a figment of your imagination? How could this champion of rationality put so much the cart before the horse and invoke a being whose being is uncertain—in the course of (of all things) trying to establish its being? No. As Karl Barth (1958) reminds us, the existence of God is never in question for Anselm, his faith is never shaken, hence whatever his proof achieves is not personal conviction. "For he had so much faith in the Divine Scriptures that he believed with unshakeable firmness of heart that there was nothing in them that in any way deviated from the path of solid truth" (*Vita* 12). All the *Proslogion,* in fact, is best understood as a dialogue with a *you* whose

3

presence is taken for granted, an interlocutor who is to participate in a decisive way in the search in which Anselm is involved; indeed, who is to make it possible, and possible for it to be successful. "Teach me to look for you, and reveal yourself to the searcher; for I cannot look for you if you don't teach me how, nor can I find you if you don't reveal yourself" (I 100 P93).[1]

A second natural solution of our worry is also barred by Barth: Anselm's concern is not proselytical, he is not trying to generate conviction in others, in the infidels. He is not, that is, trying to find a common, shared basis of beliefs and on those grounds force the unbeliever into a corner: either he comes over to Anselm's conclusions and embraces his faith, or he no longer makes sense, is shown to be conceptually confused. Anselm is not doing this because nothing like it will work. "The inexplicable possibility exists that the partner in discussion is and remains an *insipiens,* in which case all discussion with him is pointless and meaningless" (65).[2] Words by themselves can never do the trick; it is only when the *sense* of those words is grasped and accepted that conviction results, and such

[1] The attitude explored in this paragraph leaves it open that some things *other than God* (say, what time it is, or what country somebody is from) we might be able to know by ourselves, without God's help. But Anselm is very negative about knowledge of this sort: it is mostly useless, and possibly a sin. "Curiosity [one of three manifestations of *propria voluntas* (one's own will), itself the source of all evil] is the desire to inquire into those things which it is no use to know," we are told at Me47, and that includes what somebody is thinking, where he is going, or what he is doing (ibid.), how far the sun and the moon are from the earth, or how big they are (Me48), as well as any new events, spectacles, or social circumstances (Me178). It seems that the only things worth knowing are precisely those for which it is essential to get God's help. In heaven, on the other hand, we will know everything there is to know, including everything everybody did (Me280), which suggests that there is nothing wrong with the *content* of such knowledge, as much as there is with taking time to acquire this content *within our present situation*. This conclusion, in turn, directs us on the one hand to Anselm's conception of history, and on the other to his awareness of the moral and intellectual risks connected with investigative activities. The former point will surface again, if only briefly, in what follows (see note 22 of Chapter 3); the latter is going to become a central theme of this book (and eventually lead us back to the crucial relevance of the present remark; see notes 10 and 15 of Chapter 4, and the attending text).

[2] I focus more and more on the relation of Anselm to the insipiens, the fool, as this chapter develops, and eventually these words by Barth will be called into question. Maybe what is at issue is not communicating with the fool, but working with (or on) him.

grasping and accepting is not a verbal matter. Logic itself, in fact, is not verbal:

> The common term of a syllogism must be found not so much in the utterance as in the meaning. For, as nothing is accomplished if it is common verbally but not in sense: so there is nothing wrong if it is in the understanding but not in the utterance. It is the meaning that binds the syllogism together, not the words. (I 149 G43).

And making sense of words requires more enlightenment, more help on the part of The One this is all about. Thus Anselm does not even address the infidels and, though paying lip service to the military success of the Crusades,[3] discourages his fellow monks from going to Palestine, inviting them to remain instead within the peace of the monastery, not to get distracted.[4] And it is these monks who constitute his public: people, that is, who are just as convinced of the existence of God as he is, people who have already bet everything they had on that existence. Or not even (all of) these monks, maybe, because Anselm only lets his writings circulate after being subjected to long, insistent pressure,[5] which suggests that they were meant primarily for himself and, perhaps, a small circle of friends.[6] To do

---

[3] See letter 324 (V 255). See also letter 261 (IV 175), where fellow archbishop Hugh of Lyons is congratulated for having finally been able to satisfy his desire to visit Jerusalem.

[4] See IV 85–86 (where monks are prohibited from going to Jerusalem under penalty of anathema) and V 355. At Me66 Anselm uses a powerful metaphor: We are in a castle, surrounded by the enemy's army, and we are not even to look out the windows, not even if we hear our parents scream for help, for we might be hit by one of the enemy's arrows. Southern (1963, 122) emphasizes Anselm's abhorrence of the world, and then continues: "So far as we can judge, this general attitude of abhorrence overpowered all other thoughts about practical questions, even questions like the defence of the eastern Empire, the Crusade, or the reduction of freemen to servitude, which have obvious spiritual implications." See also Southern (1990, 169). This issue will receive further articulation in Chapter 2; see notes 14 and 15 there, and the attending text.

[5] See, for example, the prologue to the *Monologion* (I 7–8 M3–4) and the first chapter of the *Cur deus homo* (II 47–48 H49).

[6] Southern (1990, 115) points out that, though many of Anselm's works are in dialogue form, he "used dialogue only between friends," and "[w]hen real enemies appeared" he turned to a more defensive style. Later, his disciples Gilbert Crispin and Ralph were to make nonbelievers partners in dialogues, and this, Southern notes, "was a radical departure from the practice of Anselm" (ibid., 375).

what, if it is going to tell them nothing new? To get where, if they are already there?

A standard answer to this question is suggested by the *Proslogion*'s original title: *Fides quaerens intellectum,* faith in search of an understanding. Roughly, the answer would go like this: I *know* that God exists, that He is eternal, omnipotent, and so on. I know it from the best possible source—from revelation. No argument can add to the hold these beliefs have on me, or to their plausibility, or to their truth. Thinking otherwise would be ridiculous:

> For if others saw me, loaded with pegs and ropes and other implements with which it is customary to tie down and make steadfast swaying things, working around Mount Olympus so as to make it firm and prevent it from oscillating and being overturned when struck by somebody, it would be surprising if they could restrain themselves from laughter and mockery. (I 281; see also II 5 I10)

But still, I am a human being, and reason plays an important role for me. It gives me pleasure[7] to see how the various tenets of my faith harmonize with one another, how what I know to be the case could not possibly be otherwise, how it is not just true but also *reasonable,* logically necessary. If I could not prove *this,* I would simply have to live with my incapacity, I would have hit my boundaries and would have to accept them. Nothing would change in my beliefs, not to mention my behavior, except perhaps that I would be sad that God had chosen to be unintelligible to me. If I *can* prove it, on the other hand, I will feel my own nature somewhat vindicated, I will feel that my request for an explanation has not gone unattended, that God in His infinite wisdom has decided to give me something that *I* can lay hold of, that I can be satisfied with.[8] He's not just shown

---

[7] See, for example, I 18 M10, I 237 D135, I 273 D174, II 47 H49, II 102 H104, II 104 H105–6, II 116 H118, II 131 H134–35, and II 288 C223. In the next chapter, this theme (and some of these passages) will be brought up again and shown to have more disturbing implications than can be apparent now.

[8] There are indications, however, that even this satisfaction must not go too far. At II 276–77 C211–12 and Me123 we are told that, if the statements of faith could be proved true by experience, there would be no merit to faith itself. Though proof by reason is not mentioned in these passages, it is hard to escape the conclusion that much the same should be true of it, too. So no final rational resolution of the tension associated with religious belief can be advocated by Anselm; anxiety is to remain a constant feature of our form of life. And Anselm is quite clear about this conclusion: his letters, meditations, and prayers are full of references to the dangers of

His presence to me, He's done it in a way that I can relate to. Not that it mattered, again, for He would be present anyway and I would still be a witness to it, but it makes me feel good. "With God's protection I will never dispute how this faith could not be; with God's help I will always dispute, while believing, loving, and living, how it can be. If I can understand, I will be thankful; if I cannot, I will not toss my horns and generate disturbance, but bend my head and adore" (I 283; see also II 6–7 I11).[9]

There are important resonances to this answer. One way of looking at philosophical work in general[10] is that it consists of a perpetual struggle concerning what is *possible*. What is actual we know about: all we have to do in order to establish that is look around. We know that there are objects in space and that we have experiences of them; we know that our memory is a fairly reliable indicator of what happened (to us) in the past; and we know that some things are our duty and others are forbidden. All of this is the case, and it takes no philosophy to prove it. Philosophy enters the picture when the legitimacy of what is the case is challenged, when the issue is raised of how what is the case could possibly be the case, when arguments are voiced to the effect that what we are convinced of—and keep on being convinced of in our ordinary, nonphilosophical mode—is unintelligible, incoherent, unexplainable. You know what I am talking about: You thought you could tell what intentional behavior was, but then you put some pressure on it and the notion of an intention explodes, you no longer know what it means, you don't even know that it means anything. Or: You thought you could talk freely about relations, but then you begin to worry about whether they are internal or external or whatever, and you get confused and begin to wonder whether your talk made any sense at all.

---

feeling too safe. (A favorite line of his is: You know that few will be saved, but you don't know just how few.) As our perspective in this book changes, we will reach an understanding of this anxiety that is quite different from Anselm's official one.

[9] Southern (1990, 330) notes that this general attitude extends to Anselm's (more) practical concerns. When faced with Lanfranc's questions about the sanctity of Elphege (an object of firm belief in the English community), he "accepted the statements of faith . . . and set about finding the explanations which satisfied the demands of reason." The issue of Anselm's sensitivity to English tradition (in and by itself, and also as compared with Lanfranc's) will surface again later.

[10] For this general conception of philosophy (whose connections with Kant will emerge shortly), see Bencivenga (1987).

When challenges of this kind are posted, answering them cannot amount to pointing out the reality of intentions or relations or knowledge or duty, and claiming that because such things are real, they must be possible. Reality is beside the point, and a reference to it would be cheating. Of course these things are real, one might say, but that does not mean that we understand them, that we can conceptualize them, and it is precisely the latter feat that is required of us now. Kant put it neatly by distinguishing between empirical and transcendental concerns. Empirical concerns arise *within* experience; it is an empirical concern, for example, whether tomorrow it will rain or not, whether the lawyer knew the facts of the case, or whether it is you or I who is seeing right in this matter of the guy's promotion. Transcendental concerns, on the other hand, are *about* experience; more specifically, they are concerns about how experience is to be properly described, about the logic of the words that we use in such descriptions, about whether this logic holds water or not. Do we know what it means to know the facts of any case? or what it is to see right in any matter whatsoever? Additional data will not answer *these* questions, only rational reflection will, and if and when that happens we will not know more about the world or move more efficiently in it. The best thing we can hope for then is a sense of intellectual satisfaction, of feeling at home with ourselves, of getting the many pieces of a complicated puzzle to come together harmoniously. It's not that if they didn't our life would change; probably we would just feel a little more stupid. Or, if you will, a little less loved: by God, by fate, or whatnot.

Ultimately, there is a negative attitude toward abstract, theoretical matters involved here. Theory will not change the world, nor for that matter should it. Practice can, and must, stand on its own feet, based as it is on repetition and exercise;[11] theory only fulfills an additional, somewhat gratuitous need of ours, a need for systematicity as Kant would put it, for orderliness, for rationality. So we are best advised to do whatever else we have to do before we turn to this

---

[11] Which is especially true (and disturbing) of *evil* practice. "For instance, there are some who are consumed by the flames of greed or lust or the like, and are bound to them by evil habit. It happens occasionally that they consider their doings, weep, and promise that they will abstain from such things in the future. Why, they think that they can fly free like a bird. But because, being chained by the evil habit, they are held by the enemy, as they fly they are pulled back again into the same vices" (*Vita* 90–91).

pastime and, in any case, we are not supposed to let its outcomes infect our everyday behavior: the way we act when we act "for real," or even the way we think when thinking is an integral part of our practice. For, after all, "God often operates more through the lives of illiterates who look for what belongs to Him than through the cleverness of the literati who look for what is their own" (III 270 E301).

Anselm certainly espoused this attitude. Both as prior and abbot of Bec and as archbishop of Canterbury, he had a chance to play other than intellectual games; in fact, to influence in decisive ways the ordinary lives of a vast number of people. And you can see from his letters what his standards are when it comes to that: they are the farthest one could think from the personal search after clever arguments that characterizes him so sharply in his transcendental mode. Make no laws that it would be impossible to enforce (II 231–32 A240), watch out that your strictness not discourage people from confession (III 184 E184–85), use discretion (ibid.), make converts enjoy some comfort so that they will congratulate themselves for having chosen the true faith (V 323–24). Such is the advice he offers. In practical matters, in fact, a personal stand and a clever formulation are signs that the devil may be tempting us: "[W]e must be very careful not to follow our will too much against everybody's advice, even if it looks right to us" (III 177 E175; see also IV 139). What he stresses instead, over and over again, is the necessity for obedience. Obedience to the abbot (III 148 E138, IV 67, IV 74), though he may not be the best of all ("[I]t is better for you to sustain the burden through obedience, even to no use, than to cast it away impatiently through disobedience," III 107 E86),[12] obedience that reaches well into one's mind, and makes one not just *do* what the abbot wants, but *want* what he does (III 283 E318, IV 137, V 347), as if he were always present and could see into one's most intimate thoughts (IV 139).[13] Obedience to established rules and customs: "Preserve reli-

---

[12] In general, one must not even pass judgment on the abbot's behavior, or the whole monastery is doomed (IV 63, IV 90). And when his behavior is worthy of blame, one's criticism must always be tempered by reverence (Me164).

[13] What emerges here is a very effective rule of behavior: Don't think of anything that you could not say aloud in the presence of others. Sometimes this rule is formulated by reference to one's guardian angel (IV 135, V 275); sometimes by reference to other people (Me121), maybe the very people who would be affected by our observations (Me145); and sometimes by reference to God Himself (Me122).

giously the customs of our order which you have entered, as if they were established by God" (V 272).[14] Obedience to the archbishop, even when "the archbishop" is himself: Anselm is never as nasty in his correspondence as when Thomas, archbishop-elect of York, refuses to come and pay homage to him[15] ("I forbid you [to exercise] the priestly office, which you have undertaken by my order in my parish through my suffragan, and I enjoin you not to trust to enter in any way in any pastoral matter, until you recede from rebellion and . . . declare . . . subjection," V 420). Obedience to the Pope and to the authority of the councils: "For the whole strength of England, while I am here alone, tries to overturn me, since it cannot avert me from the obedience to the apostolic see" (IV 175). And, more than anything, obedience to God: If He has chosen to have you suffer, to have your children die, to put you in a position in which you feel that your very morality is at risk,[16] just accept it, in imitation of Christ (III 88 R140–41), since He knows better, He knows what you can stand more accurately than you do. Trust Him, abandon yourself to Him; even if you don't understand, you may be sure that He will never let anything disorderly happen in His domain.[17]

The rule intimates that there is something intrinsically subversive about the privacy of one's mind—as indeed will be argued at great length below. (By the way, note that we owe the very existence of Eadmer's biography of Anselm to an act of feigned obedience; see *Vita* 150–51.)

[14] At III 63 O198, Anselm says it is "impudent" to bear the outer signs of the monastic profession when one's life is not up to it. On the other hand, the importance of monastic customs is reaffirmed at Me77–78: there is a natural Rule, which governs one's soul, and there is a fictitious one, which governs one's external behavior. And though the fictitious Rule is no good by itself (indeed, it then makes things worse), it is highly useful to stabilize the hold of the natural one. In this connection, it is also interesting to remember Anselm's own initial difficulties in accepting monastic discipline, as reported in *Vita* 8–10: he had no trouble with the physical aspect of it, but appears to have taken longer in bringing himself into the proper frame of *mind*.

[15] Indeed, his attitude seemed unreasonable to some, for example to Bishop Samson: "I say only this, that it seems unworthy to me for you to get too angry for this reason" (V 415).

[16] See Anselm's letters to his sister Richeza and brother-in-law Burgundius (IV 107–8), to his nephew Anselm (V 259–60), and to Odo (V 384–85).

[17] See, for example, II 86 H86: "God leaves nothing unordered in His kingdom." See also II 69 H68. And see III 259 E287, where Anselm urges two relatives to extend to him the unquestioning trust ordinarily reserved for God: "I know better than [you] what is good for [people like you]."

The reason obedience is so important from a point of view that emphasizes the independence of practice from theory—indeed, the primacy of the former—is that if practice is not determined by theory, by reflecting and thinking and thereby selecting the most rational course of action, it will be most naturally conceived as determined by example, by having one's behavior match somebody else's, by a spreading of moves that comes before the establishing of any rationale for them, and nothing can work as an example unless you receive it with the proper (practical) attitude: an attitude of submissiveness and attention, of deference and respect. An obedient attitude, in sum.[18] And if this is the reason obedience is important to Anselm, it is quite natural that another major practical standard of his should be one that enters into the very definition of an example. He is, in fact, quite obsessed with the issue of setting a precedent.

Anselm spent almost half of his term as archbishop away from England, and was occasionally criticized quite harshly[19] for leaving his people and church without protection, at the mercy of their enemies, for making it more difficult for them to stand their ground. The reason he left was that Kings William and Henry requested more power in the matter of investitures, and Anselm was not ready to accept any compromise, but always stuck to the strictest interpretation of the papal injunctions. Why such an inflexible attitude, one might ask. The instructive answer is that Anselm did not want to set any wrong precedent in this area, not even by implicitly accepting, with his presence in the country, a practice he had no force to counteract:

> So it seems better to me if in my absence any tribulation (if it cannot be avoided) rages in England, than if a vicious custom is confirmed for the future by my presence and tolerance. (V 236)

---

[18] An analogy can be found in Anselm's concern for accuracy in copying texts, for which see III 155–56 E148 and III 174–75 E173 (in the latter passage he says that, when it comes to works he does not know, he would rather have only part of them, provided it was accurate, than the whole thing in a corrupted state). In all these practical matters, his emphasis is on matching a given standard (the monastic rule, the Pope's injunctions, the original text) perfectly, without residue, with absolute correctness. Given this frame of mind, it is not surprising to find that the word *rectitudo* ("correctness") plays an essential role in Anselm's definitions of both truth and justice.

[19] See V 304–5, V 308–10, and V 329–30. At V 334–35 he seems to be losing his last supporter; shortly thereafter he went back.

For if I go back in such a way that it is not clear that the king ought not to have robbed me and assailed the things of the church that had been entrusted to me, as he did, I will confirm by my example to myself and my posterity a vicious, indeed slavish and terrible custom. (V 297)

Even the nasty matter of Archbishop Thomas had precedent-setting implications ("For you must know for sure that I will work in all the ways I can, so that the church itself not lose any of its dignity during my time," V 404)—and even then he was ready to quit[20] rather than accept the disturbing novelty (V 399). To highlight his sensitivity to the issue, see how this gentle,[21] sweet man gets testy once again (it is the *only* other time he does)[22] when precedents are brought up *against him*:

[N]either in baptism nor in any ordination of mine did I promise that I would preserve the law or the custom of your father or of Archbishop Lanfranc, but the law of God and of all the orders that I entered. (V 247)

As for the priests, concerning whom the king established that they [could] have churches and wives, as they had at the time of his father and of Archbishop Lanfranc . . . , I confidently order by that authority which the archbishopric grants me. . . . (V 307)

The excitement here is well justified: when he goes against tradition, Anselm is at odds with himself. In general, he is a stark conservative; though aware of the optional character of rites and customs,[23] he wants to maintain them intact. He had seen Lanfranc try to bring

---

[20] Or to die; see V 412.

[21] References to Anselm's mild and gentle character are commonplace. See, for example, *Vita* 79 and 82, where he is regarded by some as being mild *to a fault*. One of the strongest statements can be found at Me245: "For he was, I believe, the mildest of the men who inhabited the earth at his time." In the next chapter, this mildness will be subjected to (unsympathetic) scrutiny.

[22] And again his reaction was criticized, by (usually friendly) Queen Matilda among others, and Anselm found it necessary to justify his behavior to her: "For I did not bring out anything against the king's father or Archbishop Lanfranc, men of great and religious reputation, when I pointed out that neither in [my] baptism nor in my ordinations had I promised [to adhere to] their law and customs, and I indicated that I would not contravene the law of God" (V 261). See also V 263–64.

[23] See Me77–78, summarized in note 14 above, and II 240 Sa247 (cited in Chapter 3 below).

about many changes in the English church, but from the first he could not resonate with his fellow Italian and former teacher; he seemed immediately more attuned and sympathetic to local needs and loyalties. In contrasting Anselm with Lanfranc, Richard Southern (1990, 315) says: "Anselm had not yet visited Canterbury, but he had got hold of the one thing necessary for understanding the members of the old monastic community: they wanted recognition of their saints and understanding of their tradition."

Finally, considering that an example will never be efficacious unless we repeatedly imitate it, unless we make a habit of adhering to it faithfully, down to its most minute details, it should come as no surprise that Anselm constantly stresses the importance of discipline, of never letting our behavior slip away from the mold imposed by time-honored ordinances:

> Therefore, if you want to attain your intended goal, you must proceed by saintly actions as if by steps. So arrange diligently the course of your life, not only as far as the works are concerned, but also as far as the words are; nor even only those, but also the smallest thoughts. . . . always think of what has been written most truly: "Who despises modest things, gradually falls."[24] (IV 68)

> But where the smallest excesses are not heeded, there the whole Rule is gradually dissipated and destroyed. (IV 137)

Or, in other words, "nobody becomes excellent suddenly" (Me122).

The picture that we get from these considerations is a reassuring one. Habit and tradition are to control our lives,[25] including our *re-*

---

[24] This last quote is a real favorite of Anselm's. See IV 70, IV 95, IV 135, IV 137, V 347, V 348, V 398, *Vita* 55, Me118, Me120, and Me176.

[25] An extraordinary, unwitting—indeed, extraordinary largely *because* it is unwitting—document of the effectiveness of habit is Letter 22 (III 129 E113). Here Anselm is writing to his uncles Lambert and Folcerald, the two living members of his family who had (at one point) most helped him. In the first paragraph, he insists that the passage of time and the distance between them will have no effect in diminishing his love, caused as it was by *both* the family ties *and* their generous, nurturing attitude. At this point, blood and behavior still seem on a par in determining his emotional state. But the second paragraph undercuts this equivalence. Go ahead and tell the carrier of this letter how you are, Anselm says, and hear from him all about me: he and his mother and brothers and sister have developed such *familiarity* with me, that they regard me as their own eldest brother and son. So it is the repeated experience of friendliness, *not* blood, that makes a "family" for Anselm—who, as we know, as a young man had become estranged from his own father (see *Vita* 7).

ligious lives, and rationalization is not going to make any practical difference. Just as a painter can depict Christ's glory, or a poet sing his praise, or any ordinary person admire the splendid purposiveness of all components of creation, and all of these people can rejoice in such activities without having the joy in any way strengthen their faith, much less call it into question, so does the thinker bring out, as much as he can, the mirable consistency of religious tenets. After all, the capacity for doing so is one more gift of God, and one is to make use of such gifts, if for nothing else than to keep busy in one's spare time and thus oppose the temptations that would otherwise naturally follow.

> By the grace of God you are learned; [so] turn the science that God let you acquire . . . to the love of God. (IV 271–72)

> Remove idleness from yourselves as a thing inimical to your souls, and everybody consider that we must give an account to God for each moment of our lives. Therefore, if God gives any gift to anyone for any use, they must use it, inasmuch as they have the opportunity. (IV 137)

> For which custody [of the heart] after the grace of God—as far as human effort is concerned—this advice is matchless and quite effective, to always and everywhere occupy your heart, when you are awake, either with reading or praying or psalms or some other useful thought or intention.[26] (IV 70–71)

The separation between transcendental and empirical activities is brought here to an extreme. It's not just that both are self-enclosed and self-sufficient, that they need not refer for help outside of themselves. Within the transcendental mode, there is not even any point in addressing common problems and trying to resolve them for everybody. Everybody is to resolve them for himself and, though there is tension involved, it is personal tension, the effort to satisfy a personal desire. If you do satisfy it, you can offer your solution to others, but unless they have the proper frame of mind—that is, unless they are very much like yourself—it will not work for them. The logical reconstruction of reality is a mere subjective epiphenom-

---

[26] See also IV 210. In Chapter 3, this sort of advice will be the turning point in my discussion of Anselm's "intentions."

enon that is to remain entirely private, entirely apart from the social sphere, and as such is not to raise any trouble.

But I suspect that the picture is *too* reassuring, and the situation much more intricate and problematic than it appears. To substantiate this suspicion, we need to pay closer attention to what exactly is involved (for Anselm) in the operation of understanding.

LANGUAGE TRICKS

In his reply "on behalf of the fool," Gaunilo challenges the assertion that anybody using the kinds of words Anselm uses in his proof necessarily understands what he says:

> Therefore, nor can I have that [being] in [my] thought or in [my] understanding, when I hear it said "God" or "something greater than everything," the way I have this [other] false thing [that is, a non-existent man], since whereas I could think of the latter in analogy with something true and familiar to me, the former I cannot at all think of except only according to the word, according to which only one can hardly or never think of anything true. (I 127 P117)

The issue is crucial, because Anselm (we know already) would agree that understanding is not a verbal matter, and it is also difficult because (again, as Anselm would agree) God is ultimately incomprehensible, hence it is not clear what (if anything) is understood when His name is uttered. Anselm's strategy in addressing this objection consists of two parts. On the one hand, he claims that for his proof to hold he does not need that *God* be understood, but only that a certain linguistic expression be:

> For as nothing prevents saying "ineffable," though that which is said to be "ineffable" cannot be said; and as "unthinkable" can be thought of, though that to which "unthinkable" applies cannot be thought of: so when it is said "[that] than which nothing greater can be thought," beyond doubt what is heard can be thought and understood, even if that thing cannot be thought or understood, than which a greater cannot be thought. (I 138 P133)

On the other hand, he claims that "who does not understand if a familiar language is spoken, has either an exceedingly clouded understanding or none at all [*aut nullum aut nimis obrutum . . . intel-*

15

lectum]"[27] (I 132 P125). So unless one is an idiot, or blinded by emotion, or in some other special circumstance, one should understand what is being said in a language one knows.

Anselm's first move is an effective one; it tells us that even if we understand *that* God exists, God Himself may be as far from our understanding as ever. The chances are that my "understanding" of His being will come in a purely negative form: I can*not* think of Him as nonexistent, I can*not* think of anything greater, and so on. And you don't really know a great deal concerning the nature of something if you know only what it is not. But one need not be bothered by this limitation: what is in question is not an insight into God's nature but the providing of a rational ground for the truth of a proposition. And such an operation, we know, can often be completed by taking a purely negative route—witness *reductio* arguments.[28]

Anselm's second move, on the other hand, is not quite so uncontroversial. The general structure of the situation is clear enough. Either you are not a fool, in which case if you are addressed (or you yourself speak) in a language you can handle you will make sense of what you are told (or say), or you are a fool, in which case you can go ahead and utter all sorts of nonsense: your utterances—and even your sincere commitment to them—will prove nothing about the truth of the matter. "For a thing is thought one way when a word signifying it is thought, and another way when that itself is understood, which the thing is" (I 103 P95), and hence "[n]obody indeed who understands that which God is, can think that God is not, even if he says these words in [his] heart, either with no meaning at all or with some unaccustomed meaning" (I 103–4 P95). By this bold stroke, Gaunilo's objection is turned against itself and Anselm's program seems to emerge more explicitly. He is not about to convince the fool of God's existence,[29] he *cannot,* because the fool can always

[27] See also I 285: "If [Roscelin] does not understand what he says, he is a fool." (In the final draft of this work, at II 11 I14, the reference to foolishness is deleted, and Anselm limits himself to saying that "[i]f he affirms what he does not understand, he is not to be believed.") At I 208 L106 the disciple agrees that "no one of sound mind feels otherwise." At I 17 M9 we are told that one who does not understand some obvious matters "ought not to be called a man."

[28] I will return to the significance of this negative theology in Chapter 4.

[29] Indeed, Anselm begins his response to Gaunilo with the following words: "Because it's not that 'fool' against whom I spoke in my little work who criticizes me in this work, but one who is not a fool and is a Catholic [speaking] on behalf of the fool: it can suffice for me to respond to the Catholic" (I 130 P123).

misunderstand what Anselm says. But the fool's lack of understanding is irrelevant for those who do *not* have "nullum aut nimis obrutum . . . intellectum"; for them, language works as it is supposed to, and understanding comes as a matter of course.

So far so good, then, but the problem is that we did not go very far: clear and bold as it may be, this tactic is disappointingly lacking in articulation and detail, lacking precisely in those aspects, that is, that we would normally associate with reaching an understanding of something. One would like to hear a longer story about what makes the difference between an idiot and a sensible person, between parroting words and understanding them. Even if this difference is ultimately caused by God's inscrutable will, even if it is ultimately left to Him to decide what, if anything, we should be allowed to understand, we would like to know of what the difference consists.

Forget the fool and suppose you are wise: What does *that* amount to? How do you proceed to substantiate your intellectual privilege? How do you go about reaching the *thing* Anselm talks about? In what way would it become manifest that you did reach it? In a purely ineffable one? Could you not even say anything interesting about it? So why did we get involved in this rationalization project in the first place, if we cannot even minimally explore the grounds of reason being what is in question here, and not madness?

"Many things indeed are said according to form, which are not according to the thing," Anselm says (I 250 D149), and then again: "Many other things, too, which are not something, are similarly said [to be] something according to the form of speech, since we speak of them as of existing things" (I 250–51 D150). And when the disciple throws up his hands and laments, "I cannot contradict the reasoning, but linguistic usage does not agree" (I 253 D152), the teacher responds, "No wonder. For many things are said improperly in ordinary discourse; but when one has to inquire into the kernel of truth, it is necessary to discern the disturbing impropriety as much as possible and as much as the thing requires" (ibid.).[30] Along

---

[30] See also I 164 G64. At Me347 F17, interesting details are offered on this "improper" use of words. "It seems to me," Anselm says, "whenever either a noun or a verb is attributed to a thing improperly, that the thing to which it is attributed is either similar to or a cause or an effect or a genus or a species of [or, to make a long story short, somehow related to] the thing of which it is said properly." So the "impropriety" of language is its capacity to "spread" along the classical axes of

these lines, Anselm's quest for intelligibility becomes a practice of linguistic elucidation; his concern with going beyond words and reaching things articulates itself as a project of finding *better* words, more accurate words, less confusing ones.

There are all sorts of problems with the language we speak, Anselm thinks. To begin with, we have a tendency to be sloppy and to use inappropriate expressions even when appropriate ones are at hand. Occasionally, to make things more precise, we need to make the structure of our speech substantially more complicated; for example, to rewrite as a counterfactual what appears at first as a simple sentence in the indicative: "But when we say that injustice makes a robbery, or blindness makes a man fall into a pit, by no means is it to be understood that injustice or blindness do anything; but that if justice were in the will and sight in the eye, neither the robbery nor the fall into the pit would occur" (I 274 D175; see also II 64 H63–64 and II 146 Vi150–51). But often the remedy is much more easily available: "For by frequent usage we say that we cannot [do] something, not because it is impossible for us, but because we cannot [do] it without difficulty" (I 218 L116; see also I 105 P97, II 257 C192–93, and II 278 C214).

Second, language is ambiguous: "Since then [these phrases] do not always have the same sense . . . one must inquire more diligently . . ." (I 18 M11). "We say 'make' [*facere,* which also means "to do"] in several ways. For we say 'make' when we make something happen, and when we can make it not happen and don't do it" (I 263 D162; see also I 34 M30, I 162 G61, I 182 Ve83, I 234 D132, I 265 D165, and II 62 H61). Which problem becomes especially troublesome when we realize that there might be an ambiguity between anything we mean by an expression and what *God* means by it:

> Therefore in what way are You both merciful and not merciful, Lord, if not because You are merciful according to us, and not according to Yourself? Indeed You are [merciful] according to our sense, and are not according to Yours. (I 106 P98)

---

metaphor and metonymy, that very capacity which for some is its most essential feature (see chapter 8 of Bencivenga, 1989); and *correcting* the impropriety means resisting the spreading—and opposing its subversive character. More about this in Chapter 3.

[T]he supreme essence is so much above and beyond every other nature that, if something is said of It by words that are common to other natures, the sense is by no means common. (I 76 M74; see also I 44 M41)

Third, language is also misleading, in that perfectly grammatical expressions appear on closer inspection to give us the wrong picture of the situation; one that is so wrong, in fact, as to run exactly counter to what the truth of the matter is. More specifically, it often happens that language suggests that things exist when they do not, or that things are done when nothing is. Sometimes, the problem arises with single words: "But the fourth one is improperly called power. For what usually impedes sight is not said to give the power of seeing when it does not impede, if not because it does not take it away" (I 213 L111). And sometimes it arises with whole sentences: "Therefore when I say that I ought to be loved by you, it is not said as if I owed something, but because you ought to love me. . . . As when it is said: Hector could be vanquished by Achilles. . . . There was no power in the one who could be vanquished, but in the one who could vanquish" (I 188 Ve89; see also I 217 L115, I 254 D153, II 123 H125–26, and II 128–29 H132).

Finally, language is incomplete: it does not cover reality; it leaves things large and small totally unaccounted for, speechless; it forces us to stretch our resources, to use whatever comes close, inappropriate as it may be.

And because we do not have a present passive participle for the verb "to preserve" which I am using here, instead of the present we can use the past passive participle of the same verb. We have the very well known practice of using past passive participles instead of the present ones that Latin does not have, as it does not have past participles of active and neuter verbs, and instead of the past which it does not have it uses the present, as when I say of someone: What he learned studying and reading, he does not teach if not forced. That is: What he learned while he studied and read, he does not teach unless one forces him. (I 196 Ve98)

Which last feature is, again, especially problematic (and relevant) when it comes to speaking of God:

So if someone wants to speak to another, what will he say the Father and Son and their Spirit are three of, unless perhaps, compelled by

19

the lack of a properly fitting noun, he chooses one of those nouns which cannot be said plurally in the supreme essence, to signify what cannot be said by an adequate noun . . . ? (I 85–86 M84–85; see also IV 96)

But the same apostle, in order to show that he had not put down those verbs on account of their temporal significance, announced even those things which are future by a verb in the past tense. For it was not yet the case, of those He foreknew were still to be born, that He temporally "called" them, "justified" them, "magnified" them. Wherefrom it can be known that, because of the lack of a verb signifying the eternal presence, he used verbs signifying the past; since those things which are past in time are wholly immutable in analogy with the eternal present. For indeed the things temporally past are more similar to the eternal present than those [temporally] present in this respect, that those which are [in the eternal present] can never not be present, just as those which are past in time can never not be past, but those which are present in time and pass become not present. (II 254 C189–90; see also I 267 D167)

Thus, in the end, we want to be extremely careful when it comes to language;[31] to become sensitive to the different nuances suggested by the humblest parts of speech ("So for this reason I think it can be said more appropriately that one must believe in it rather than toward [ad] it," I 84 M83; "[I]t is better to say that it is everywhere [than in every place] . . . [and] that it is always than at every time," I 42 M39; "[B]y this monosyllabic utterance, that is, 'one,' one does not understand a human [person] more than just any person," II 198 S206), to struggle for the proper reading of a genitive case ("But it is certain that He is not said [to be] 'the spirit of God' in the sense of possession, as when a horse or a house is said [to be] 'of someone.' . . . Nor is He said [to be] 'the spirit of God' in the sense of a member of God, as a hand or a foot of a man," II 209–10 S219) or of a gender termination ("[M]ore could be said about the trinity and plu-

---

[31] Anselm's most sustained and systematic effort in linguistic analysis is the incomplete work reprinted at Me334–51 F3–29 and analyzed by Henry (1967). There is nothing much in this work that cannot be learned from Anselm's other, theological, works, but it is highly significant that (except for the early *De grammatico*) he chose to utilize his logical skills only in theological contexts while leaving this work incomplete and unpublished. It suggests that logic's only worth is as a weapon to fight against the enemies of the faith—a suggestion I will explore below.

rality, [such as] how the Word is *unum* [one thing] but not *unus* [one person] with the Father, and *unus* but not *unum* with the man whom It assumed," IV 97), and in general to pay a lot of attention to all traits of this elusive medium, even those considered trivial, even when for all we know they might *be* trivial.[32]

Anselm's attitude toward language as expounded above has clear analogues in contemporary thought. Gottlob Frege (1892a, 168–69) complains as follows about language's misleading character (with specific reference to its delusive evocation of unreal entities, hence in the general spirit of Anselm's remarks concerning, say, a "power" that is not a power):

> Now languages have the fault of containing expressions which fail to designate an object (although their grammatical form seems to qualify them for that purpose) because the truth of some sentence is a pre-requisite. . . . This arises from an imperfection of language, from which even the symbolic language of mathematical analysis is not altogether free; even there combinations of symbols can occur that seem to mean something but (at least so far) do not mean anything.

And in (1897a, 239) Frege notes: "[M]ost logicians, misled by language, take the words 'some numbers' in the sentence 'some numbers are prime numbers' together, and treat their meaning as a logical subject of which the property of being a prime number is predicated, just as it is predicated of say the number 2 in the sentence 'two is a prime number'" (compare it with Anselm's search for the proper analysis of "I ought to be loved by you"). And, again, in (1906a, 177) Frege points out that words are often lacking for expressing certain senses, and inappropriate words are then used: "So language brands a concept as an object, since the only way it can fit the designation for a concept into its grammatical structure is as a proper name. But in so doing, strictly speaking it falsifies matters" (see also 1906b, 193). Thus, in general, "on thorough investigation

---

[32] Southern (1990, 75) says of Anselm that "[w]ithout doubt, he had the finest sensibility for words and sounds, and a strong conviction that human speech reflects the original ordering of the universe." (See also the passage from Southern, 1963, 352, quoted in note 13 of Chapter 4.) Some evidence of the sensibility referred to here is provided by Anselm's puns in his letters. See III 211 E222 (*militia/malitia*), IV 159 and IV 160 (*Clementia/clementia*), V 263 (*pravum/parvum*), and V 322 (*Anglos/angelos*). See also the near-Heideggerian etymology at Me40 (*Superbia/supra quam debeat*).

it will be found that the obstacle is essential, and founded on the nature of our language; that we cannot avoid a certain inappropriateness of linguistic expression; and that there is nothing for it but to realize this and always take it into account" (1892b, 194).

On the other hand, language is all we have: "[W]e cannot come to an understanding with one another apart from language, and so in the end we must always rely on other people's understanding words, inflexions, and sentence-construction in essentially the same way as ourselves" (ibid., 184–85; remember Anselm's remark that, after all, those who do not have an "obrutum intellectum" will understand when addressed in a language they speak). So a tension arises: "These investigations are especially difficult because in the very act of conducting them we are easily misled by language; by language which is, after all, an indispensable tool for carrying them out" (1924, 266). And one is forced, against one's will, to turn one's attention from the subject matter to the medium, and to become involved in questions one would gladly forget about, if only one could: "I am compelled to occupy myself with language although it is not my proper concern here" (1918, 360n). Indeed, these questions tend to take an inordinate amount of one's time and energy, and to dislocate into an indeterminate future the long sought-for addressing of one's "proper concern":

> If our language were logically more perfect, we would perhaps have no further need of logic, or we might read it off from the language. But we are far from being in such a position. Work in logic just is, to a large extent, a struggle with the logical defects of language, and yet language remains for us an indispensable tool. Only after our logical work has been completed shall we possess a more perfect instrument. (1915, 252)

Until that time, the logician, "[i]nstead of following grammar blindly, . . . ought rather to see his task as that of freeing us from the fetters of language" (1897b, 143). "It is rather the task of this science [that is, of logic] to purify what is logical [*das Logische*][33] of all that is alien and hence of all that is psychological, and to free

[33] The English edition translates *das Logische* as "logic," but the translation "what is logical" seems preferable on (at least) the following two counts: (a) "logic" already translates *Logik* (which also occurs in this passage), and (b) the subsequent expression *das Psychologische* is translated "all that is psychological." See Frege (1969, 160–61).

thinking from the fetters of language by pointing out the logical imperfections of language" (ibid., 149).

Alfred Tarski (1935) sees the problems posed by language from a different standpoint. It's not so much that language subjects our thought to strictures from which logic is to liberate us but, rather, that language is *too* free and needs some regimenting if any serious work is to be done with it.

> A characteristic feature of colloquial language (in contrast to various scientific languages) is its universality. It would not be in harmony with the spirit of this language if in some other language a word occurred which could not be translated into it; it could be claimed that "if we can speak meaningfully about anything at all, we can also speak about it in colloquial language." (164)

And this universality is a problem. On the one hand, it makes it "hopeless" to reach "a general structural definition of a true sentence," since "this language is not something finished, closed, or bounded by clear limits" (ibid.). On the other, such a lack of clear organization and definite boundaries "leads inevitably to confusions and contradictions" (267), and hence forces one "to undertake the thankless task of a reform of this language," which means (at least) "to define its structure, to overcome the ambiguity of the terms which occur in it, and finally to split the language into a series of languages of greater and greater extent" (ibid.).

But if Tarski's metaphors are different from Frege's, the message conveyed is essentially the same: the problem of (colloquial) language may be one of richness, there may be too much potential there for our (and its own) good, but in practice we end up with the same sort of embarrassment. We cannot function properly with this unlimited means of expression, and hence *we* are limited in the use we can make of it, as people might be with an overbearing, genial, but somewhat inconsistent person. If we want to operate effectively in this area, and not be deluded by our forms of speech, language will have to be modified: careful distinctions and limits will have to be drawn *and* maintained.

There is, of course, a more optimistic view of the whole thing.[34] One need not think, that is, that (ordinary) language is hopeless and

---

[34] And one closer to Anselm. See, for example, the passage from I 253 D152 quoted on p. 17 above.

that the best thing we can do is get rid of it in favor of something clearer and more serviceable. One can think of the definition of a new, artificial jargon (not as an attempt at bypassing language altogether, but) as a detour through more comprehensible structures that will eventually make us able to understand language, the very language with which we started. Russell's talk of uncovering the "logical form" of our statements goes in this direction, and so does, even more explicitly, Carnap's program in (1934). What Carnap calls "word-languages" are just too complicated to be studied without first developing adequate analytical tools, "just as a physicist would be frustrated were he from the outset to attempt to relate his laws to natural things—trees, stones, and so on" (8), but when the tools are developed we will be able to return to word-languages and, as in the physicist's case, be "in a position to analyze into suitable elements the complicated behaviour of real bodies, and thus to control them" (ibid.).

This ambitious plan constitutes the theoretical underpinning of elementary logic courses; truth tables are not just a game, it is suggested there—once you learn them they actually help you think straight and talk sense. Clearly, no collection of such courses will ever establish the point; the merging of logic and linguistics envisioned by some[35] belongs to an indeterminate future, and it takes faith to hold on to such a vision. But the faith is not uncommon, and not irrelevant to Anselm. With practice and exercise, the student will be made to see through the traps of language, his intellect will no longer be impeded by ambiguities and confusion, and the true structure of things will emerge from under the veil of linguistic distortion.

TEACHING RATIONALITY

I started out, in the first section, contrasting repetitive, efficacious, "blind" practices with the self-indulgent luxury of reaching a transparent understanding of our beliefs. There I depicted these two sorts of activities as being entirely disconnected, and their laws as having no overlap. But in fact, insofar as they are both *activities* of sorts, there is bound to be an overlap, and this issue began to emerge in

---

[35] See Massey (1975a,b) and Bencivenga (1979).

the second section, where it was pointed out that rationalization is itself a practice, a concrete project, something you *do* over the course of (some) time, pliable and evanescent as the object of your practice (language, that is) might be. And if it is a practice, if it substantiates itself as a set of moves, it must arise and spread the same way all practices do: by repetition and example.

Many of Anselm's statements agree with this suggestion and help articulate it. Thus, at the beginning of the *Monologion,* he brings out immediately the practical nature of his enterprise: his brethren have heard him phrase his meditations before, and have asked him to put some of them in writing "as an example of meditation for them"[36] (I 7 M3). Later, while writing the *Proslogion,* Anselm refers to his earlier effort as to "a little work [written] as an example of meditating on the reason of faith" (I 93 P89); in fact, *Exemplum meditandi de ratione fidei* was the original title of that little work.[37] To generate examples of this kind, one has to put oneself in the proper thinking and behavioral mode, to play a role as it were, and let none of one's (other) knowledge and skills interfere with that role. Thus the *Proslogion's* pretense will be that it is written "under the guise of one trying to raise his mind to contemplating God and seeking to understand what he believes" (I 93–94 P89), and a similar assumption is made in the *Cur deus homo*: "Since in this investigation you are assuming the role of those who will believe nothing unless it is first rationally demonstrated, I want to agree with you that we accept nothing even minimally discordant in God, and reject not even a minimal reason, unless a greater one is opposed" (II 67 H66). An agreement that Anselm tends to forget, and a role about which he must be occasionally reminded—thus, near the end of the work, Boso urges: "Have you forgotten what I objected to your excuses at the beginning of this discussion of ours, that is, that you not do what I asked for the learned, but for me and for those asking with me?" (II 122 H124).

Boso's prompting follows a natural line of interpretation of Anselm's practice. His painstaking role-playing has primarily pedagogical significance: To be maximally effective, the teacher has to

---

[36] Note that the word "example" does not occur in Hopkins and Richardson's edition of the *Monologion.*

[37] See also I 236 D134, where the disciple says: "I want you to show me what you say by an example."

put himself in the student's shoes, not despise his simpleminded queries and objections, and be willing to take it easy when it comes to the unfolding of the argument. No high-flying fancy is to be allowed here, no erudite display, not even extraordinary pity. The objective is talking *to,* not *at,* one's audience, and sharing their no-nonsense, somewhat mediocre and obtuse attitude.[38]

The brethren soliciting the *Monologion,* indeed, wanted it "to be in a plain style and [to use] commonplace arguments and a simple discussion," and insisted "that [he] not disdain to respond to [any] simple and almost fatuous objections that occurred [to him]" (I 7 M3). Anselm is going to oblige. Later in the work he assures us that "[he wants] to neglect and disregard no objection however simple and almost fatuous occurring [to him] as he inquires," and that he will proceed in such a way that "every obstacle however modest having been removed, any slow understanding could easily approach the things heard" (I 19 M12). And he is convinced that it will work: "I believe that he can to a large extent persuade himself of these same things, if he has even an ordinary intelligence," so that "reason guiding and him following, he proceed rationally toward those things which he irrationally ignores" (I 13–14 M5).[39]

This emphasis on humble, example-based—indeed, acting-like—educational technique sheds new light on how Anselm is to relate to the fool, and on that proper understanding of language that differentiates the two. Such proper understanding may be not (just) a

---

[38] Anselm's pedagogical drive is best expressed in his constant concern (and preference) for the training of young people; see IV 40–41, IV 55, IV 56, IV 211, IV 229, and V 299. In *Vita* 20–21 he is reported as giving a rationale for this concern: Youth is like a piece of wax of the right consistency for the impress of a seal, neither too hard nor too soft, hence it is maximally capable of profiting from education. Against this background, it is somewhat surprising to see Anselm say to one of his former pupils: "[Y]ou know how annoying it always was for me to practice grammar with the boys" (III 180 E180, in a context in which he insists on the value of this practice and advises the young man to take advantage of some other teacher's presence). Some tension is clearly at work here, between Anselm's general enthusiasm for pedagogy and his disinclination for the details of indoctrinating the young. A similar tension emerges concerning the other side of the present coin: patient, daily "impressing" of the educational seal versus singleminded, individualistic, heroic efforts. Anselm discourages the latter; see IV 86, where he urges a monk named Richard to temper his excessive abstinence and sacrifice, and also V 393–94, *Vita* 60, Me94, and Me99. But, as I point out early in the next chapter, *he* does not seem to take his own advice in this matter.

[39] See *Vita* 54–57, which reports on Anselm's pedagogical skill and success.

matter of blissful grace, and idiocy not (necessarily) an irrevocable sentence; there may be ways of working toward some partial reconciliation here, of bringing the extremes closer. Clearly, the fool's *obrutus intellectus* is in part a curse. He may be told all the right things and never make (the right) sense out of them. His gaze is not going to pierce through enigmas the way the young Christ's—or even the young Anselm's[40]—did. But that is not the end of the matter. His poor sight can be helped, language's many tricks can be patiently pointed out to him, one can take him by the hand and show him, in words that he can handle, how to slowly conquer (some of) his limitations, how to painfully stretch his means[41] and acquire more subtlety, more acumen, more understanding.[42]

In fact, this sort of work has an even greater significance. It's not just that if we ever ran into a fool we would know what to do; *all of us* are fools to some extent, and the perpetual search for transparency that Anselm suggests, the reading of, and meditating on, the "examples" he and others offer on how to conduct this search, and the stubborn confrontation with the opacity of language that so much of the search comes down to, are going to contribute to making us— *all of us*—less foolish. Rational enlightenment will not come at once to humankind, the way revelation did; it will, rather, consist of an unending effort, of a constant struggle, never quite victorious but still relentlessly progressing, against all the confusion in which we are immersed, all the nonsense that our weak, sinful race has been burdened with, probably as a punishment for its sin. "Our present

---

[40] See the vision reported in the *Vita* (4–5) and later confirmed (see *Vita* 14).

[41] At Me119, foolishness is associated with negligence; more specifically, with delaying indefinitely work that would be best done now. And at Me84 it is considered foolish to give up on the custody of one's innocence after a few failures—as one gives up on a medicine after failing to be cured at once. The suggestion is, clearly, that a condition for *not* being a fool is getting involved in painstaking, disciplined work of some sort.

[42] In this process, it is crucial to avoid isolation and to listen to others: each of us can help his fellow humans deal with their blind spots. See III 123–24 E106, III 177 E175–76, IV 119, IV 120, IV 139, IV 169, and IV 205. But note a problem with this strategy, which emerges at III 270 E301: Anselm had urged Fulk to accept the bishopric of Beauvais, largely because he was worried about giving too much weight to his own concerns in the presence of a general consensus, but now he has come to the conclusion that he was right and the general consensus wrong. A similar problem, of course, arose in connection with Anselm's own acceptance of the (arch)bishopric.

27

life is a journey. For as long as man lives, all he does is travel" (V 365). One is always on the move, and one is never going to reach one's destination, so the only acceptable course of action is to continue to strive for it: "[I]t is necessary that those who always want to avoid failure, always strive to do better" (III 274 E307; see also IV 69). And our limited powers are never going to be, just by themselves, enough of an excuse: "I agree that no man can completely disclose in this life so great a secret," insists the implacable Boso, "and I am not asking that you do what no man can do, but as much as you can. For you will convince [me] more that in this matter deeper reasons are hidden, if you show me that you see some [reason], than if you prove yourself to understand no reason in it by saying nothing" (II 117 H119).

This pedagogical dimension of the search for better words has not escaped contemporary logicians—in practice if not always in theory. Dana Scott (1973) acknowledges that "[h]ow one *teaches* the knack of uncovering [hidden] assumptions is another question and a serious one" (244). The answer to this question is to be found in any of the swarm of manuals that have proliferated in these days in which "there seems to be a chance for formal logic to have a wider audience" (ibid., 245). No subject in philosophy, and few subjects anywhere, are treated through more examples and exercises than this one. The conceptual content of an introductory logic course could be spelled out in a couple of pages; the rest of what happens in class and out of it is practice: the painstaking quest for hidden assumptions in arguments found in newspapers (try the letters to the editor first), paraphrase of ordinary English into artificial jargons, and construction of truth tables, trees, derivations, sequents, or whatever. By this process, all participants will become enlightened to the ambiguities of disjunction, sensitive to the chasm between indicative and subjunctive conditionals, wise to slippery-slope paradoxes, and proficient in the not-so-trivial task of proving Peirce's Law. Which, eventually, will make not just for better words, but for better people as well—intellectually better, at least. "The logic books contain warnings against logical mistakes arising from the ambiguity of expressions," says Frege (1892a, 169), and continues:

> I regard as no less pertinent a warning against apparent proper names without any meaning. . . . This lends itself to demagogic abuse as easily as ambiguity—perhaps more easily. "The will of the people"

can serve as an example; for it is easy to establish that there is at any rate no generally accepted meaning for this expression.

Or listen to Wittgenstein (1958, 26):

> Now a definition often clears up the *grammar* of a word. And in fact it is the grammar of the word "time" which puzzles us. We are only expressing this puzzlement by asking a slightly misleading question [as Augustine and others have done], the question: "What is . . . ?" This question is an utterance of unclarity, of mental discomfort, and it is comparable with the question "Why?" as children so often ask it.

Or to Reichenbach (1951, 316–17):

> Although the scientific philosopher refuses to give ethical advice, he is willing, in following his program, to discuss the nature of ethical advice and thus to extend his method of clarification to the study of the logical side of this human activity. . . . Since men are often none too clear about their goals and do many things without reflecting about their own intentions, the adviser may sometimes be able to tell a man what he "really wants." . . . This form of advice is the most efficient one.

Keeping in mind that this operation of liberating oneself from discomfort and confusion and opacity is not going to be easy:

> The present volume, at any rate, is written by one who does not look upon the subject as an amusement. He will endeavor to make the doctrine present an exterior as little odious as possible, to correspond with its inward divine beauty, and to harmonize with the deep happiness the study brings. But he will not attempt to prostitute the science to the purposes of the purposeless. In order to enjoy it, it will be needful to have one's heart set on something remote from enjoyment. (Peirce, 1965, 2:9).

Where Anselm, of course, agrees:

> It must be known that, as the earth brings forth without any human care innumerable herbs and trees, without which human nature prospers or by which it is even killed, whereas those [herbs and trees] that are most necessary to us in order to nourish life [it does] not [bring forth] without great labor and a tiller and seeds: similarly human hearts without instruction, without zeal, germinate spontaneously, as

it were, thoughts and volitions useless or even harmful to salvation, whereas those [thoughts and volitions] without which we do not make progress toward the soul's salvation [human hearts] by no means conceive or germinate without a seed of their kind and laborious cultivation. (II 270 C206)

But wait. Let's not get carried away by rhetoric here; let's stop and reconsider the facts. Language may well be misleading, and practice may make us more sensitive to (some of) its traps; but if the relevant operation is an interminable one, and the sensuous character of words is going to remain in the way, what real advantage is this partial enlightenment going to be? In fact, how do we know that by stigmatizing certain aspects of language as "traps" we are not losing vital instruments of expression and falling into subtler, more sophisticated, and so far remote and unthreatening, sorts of idiotic confusion? How do we know that our clever enemy is not turning our own cleverness against us, and making us lose our souls in the process? That we are not being outsmarted by our own smart moves?

To see the problem from a different angle, take the following lead. If I get on the road to Paris or Moscow, I may never get there, but since it is *possible* to get there (after all, people do), I know *what it is* that I am doing: traveling toward Paris or Moscow. I may get sidetracked in the process and find myself in Rio; that will amount to interrupting, or being forced away from, my traveling toward Paris or Moscow, and the moment I get back on track (if ever) I will have resumed my original course of action. If, on the other hand, I get on the road to Toontown, I can't say that I know what I am doing. Traveling toward Toontown it can't be, because there is no such place.[43] Could it perhaps be *trying* to travel there? It sounds promising at first, but when questions are asked the promise thins out. How does one try to do something like that? What sorts of moves are involved in this practice? I can make sense of trying to travel to Paris because I know what it is to travel there, but what sense can I make of trying to do the impossible? So the conjecture naturally arises that, contra the appearances and my own "internal reports,"

[43] Long after this passage was first written, Walt Disney Co. opened a new section of Disneyland called "Toontown." So I must hasten to add that here I refer to the Toontown of the 1988 movie *Who Framed Roger Rabbit,* that is, to a city inhabited by cartoon characters, not to its counterpart in Anaheim.

I am really doing something else: escaping my responsibilities, getting away from unpleasant company, or finding a silly excuse to exercise. It's not the only way of looking at the matter, of course; not everybody will endorse this "hermeneutics of suspicion."[44] But it is a natural way, and a natural suspicion.

The same way is open, and the same suspicion natural, with the enlightenment promised by Anselm—and by his fellow logicians. At Me168 he is reported as saying that "nobody will reach perfection except those who will try to arrive at even greater things than they can reach." But this statement is misleading; it makes it sound as if perfection were like Paris, something actually reached by some, to which (some) others will only be able to get a little closer. And we know that this is not the case. Perfection is not an option in our present, earthly condition—not moral perfection, and not even *logical* perfection. Figural, symbolic, and ultimately inadequate representations of matters of faith are an inevitable component of our form of life (II 228 A236–37). Every one of us is "an exile from [his] Lord" (III 8 O97), and can't even properly express in words his own mental states: it "cannot be done" (III 174 E172). Even if we were faced by what we are missing, still we could not do it justice in our speech. In Anselm's dialogue on the custody of the inner man, the character called "Desire of Eternal Life" concludes the report of his vision by saying: "Here I told you few things among those which I saw in heaven. For neither could I say exactly how I saw [them], nor could I see [them] just as they were" (Me360). We see the things that matter only "in an enigma" (Me148), that is, much like in a picture (ibid.); and the picture of a man, Anselm would say, simply *is not* a man (II 142 Vi146).

But then, if logical transparency is out of the question, do we even know what it is *to strive after* it? In his sermon on the joys of eternity, Anselm brings up the speed of the sun's rays to make what he says about our speed and agility in heaven not sound impossible (Me276), but when it comes to the sort of health the blessed will experience he is at a loss: "I don't see what example I could bring so that it be understood what it is like" (Me277). And he realizes that he has a problem: What can he say of those people, "to establish whether they are or are not healthy" (ibid.)? The usual criteria fail, and all we are

---

[44] For the sense of this expression, see the discussion of the three great "masters of suspicion" (Marx, Nietzsche, and Freud) in Ricoeur (1965).

left with is an appeal to faith. We must never stop believing in this perfect health of the blessed, though literally we don't know *what* we believe: it is "ineffable" (Me278). For, ultimately, understanding depends on experiencing (IV 139). So, if what we can't possibly experience we can make no sense of, what sense does it make, again, to strive after it? How shall we read Anselm's encouragement to try for what is out of our reach?[45] How shall we read his insistence that, unless we keep on moving forward, we will be stepping back? Which direction is forward here? How are we supposed to know? How can we determine a course if we don't know its target? Aren't we perhaps, in this case as in the previous one of traveling to Toontown, really doing something else when we so "strive"? And what could that be?

In the next two, central, chapters of this book I will look for answers to these questions.[46] Anselm's program, both insofar as it typifies a logician's program and insofar as it bears the special mark of attempting to make us think straight*er* about the Ineffable Master of all things, will be subjected first to unsympathetic criticism and then to that sort of salvaging which may make some regret the execution squad. This way, however, what I perceive as its significance will finally be allowed to emerge, and within the context thus reconstructed a place will also be found for rational reflection upon That One, than which a greater cannot be thought.

---

[45] I 137–38 P133 legitimizes (by a quote from St. Paul) extrapolation from visible to invisible things, and IV 75 tells us that "[God] judges good every believer who in his condition tries to reach perfection."

[46] Then, in Chapter 4, I will also consider another related question: Why is it that, if indeed Anselm is doing something else, his activity is *described* as the (impossible) search for something out of reach?

CHAPTER 2

The Program Criticized

We can lean on a rock, we can feel a firm foothold
Against the perpetual wash of tides of balance of forces . . .
The rock of God is beneath our feet. . . .
Our lord, our Archbishop returns. And when the Archbishop returns
Our doubts are dispelled. Let us therefore rejoice.

INFLEXIBLE REASON

So FAR, the game of rationality has been represented as a harmless, entertaining one. A game with rules, of course—not a free-for-all sort of anarchistic outburst but a disciplined, serious, painstaking pursuit of an elusive prize, of an absconding insight into the reality of things. Still a game, though; nothing is to be earned here except pleasure and peace of mind, no conceivable function performed except keeping the monks busy with other than devilish thoughts and intents. But now that doubts have been raised concerning this good-natured, reassuring picture, and the suggestion made that, given *how* elusive the prize is, and how absconding the insight, the playful monks could possibly be after some other business, we must be on the lookout for some cracks, some gestures that don't quite square with the official ideology of the operation. There, if anywhere, we should be treated to a glimpse into what other story could be told, what else could be hidden under these saintly "childish" concerns.

A first element that gives us pause is the emotional intensity associated with the search.[1] Anselm's description of it reaches its peak in the proem to the *Proslogion*:

And as I turned my thought frequently and zealously to this [goal], and sometimes it seemed to me that what I was looking for could be attained, sometimes it completely escaped the acuity of my mind: eventually in desperation I wanted to stop, as from the search of a

---

[1] Southern (1990, 217) says: "As always in Anselm, the intensely emotional appeal is inseparable from the most rigorous logic."

33

thing which it was impossible to find. But when I wanted to wholly remove that thought from me, so that it could not impede my mind, by occupying it without use, from other things in which I could succeed: then it began to force itself more and more [on me] who was unwilling and defended [against it], with a certain importunity. Then one day, as I was wearying by vehemently resisting its importunity. . . . (I 93 P89)[2]

With all due respect, this describes an addiction, much like a compulsive gambler's or a bulimic's or whatever your favorite example is, with attempted withdrawals and anxiety attacks and the sense of wasting oneself and one's time and the incapacity to get rid of this monkey by one's own willpower alone and all the rest of it.[3] Of course, what follows the dots in the quote is the description of a miraculous resolution of the problem, but since admittedly there is no human control on miracles, all one is left with, on this side of omnipotence, is the addiction. And how is that to be reconciled with the peaceful, innocent playfulness that is supposed to be at work here?

A natural answer to this question is that the game went too far. You are not a gambler if you play some poker with your friends once a month, or take a trip to Vegas every now and then; such distractions, in fact, may ultimately work to your benefit, and keep you away from more dangerous occupations—and more destabilizing distractions. But you will be walking a thin line, and unless you check yourself carefully you might end up taking a trip too many to Vegas, and go broke and mortgage the farm. Still, this is only a game; your obsession is no evidence that its point has grown larger, or indeed that it has grown a point at all. It is only evidence that something that has no point (except, again, to provide you with much-needed relaxation) has gotten out of hand and acquired control over all sorts of other things that *have* a point. Similarly, Anselm came dangerously close to emotional, and possibly moral, bank-

---

[2] Importunity will become a central character in Chapter 3.

[3] For behavior strongly reminiscent of addiction, see also *Vita* 80–81. By his own testimony, Anselm had been "weaned" early from the affairs of the world, to the point of getting weary and sick if he was forced to attend to them. When this happened, his disciples "drew him out of the crowd and proposed to him some question from the Divine Scripture [thus restoring] his body and spirit to the usual state as if cured by a wholesome antidote."

ruptcy here, and good for him (and possibly us) that miraculous intervention got him out of trouble. It's not so different from Christ's freeing Mary Magdalene from her seven demons, or from the ghosts' scaring Scrooge into doing charity work.

This answer might appease us for a moment, but it won't take long before a new worry surfaces. Why does Anselm, if indeed he is aware of the dangers of becoming too involved in mental games, continue to indulge in them till the end of his life?[4] Why does he, late in life, recommend daily intellectual exercise to his nephew and namesake? (See IV 210, V 260.) Why does he put in Boso's mouth, in the *Cur deus homo,* words clearly suggesting that rational inquiry is a *duty* for the believer: "[I]t seems negligence to me if, once we are confirmed in the faith, we don't make an effort to understand what we believe" (II 48 H50)? Does he expect liberating miracles to come as a matter of course? Why doesn't he play it more cautiously here, as he does in other, more practical matters? We know already that he sternly forbids monks to follow up that other obsession of taking the way to Jerusalem, calling it a "disordered wandering" that makes one fall into "confusion and damnation" (IV 85), and wants them instead to stick around and carry out their ordinary duties while enforcing "stability before God in the monastery" (V 355). We know that he doesn't even want them to leave the monastery where they happen to be, and insists that any suggestion to the contrary may be the devil's work.[5] So why this strange leniency

---

[4] An impressive document of Anselm's commitment to intellectual activity can be found in the *Vita*. He is lying on his bed, where he is to die three days later, and his friends tell him that soon he will be at God's court. Anselm answers: "And indeed if His will is in this, I will gladly obey His will. But if He preferred that I still remain among you at least until I can resolve the question about the origin of the soul that I am revolving in my mind, I would accept that gratefully, since I don't know whether anybody is going to solve it once I am dead" (142). The *Vita* also suggests that Anselm became a monk because of his inclination to literary studies, not the other way around. Lanfranc was, after all, the best teacher he could find, and after working day and night on books for a while, he realized that his life as a monk would not be much different, and might earn him higher (celestial) rewards (8ff).

[5] The most important document of this attitude is the letter to Lanzo (III 144–48 E133–37), to be discussed in some detail in Chapter 3. See also III 122–24 E105–7, where Anselm advises a monk named Henry not to go to Italy to relieve his sister from servitude; IV 73–74, where he discourages a monk named Richard from fulfilling a vow made before he committed himself to the monastic profession ("I advise you and instruct you . . . to remain quiet and settled in the resolution which

toward the addictive vagaries of the intellect? This less than stern attitude toward a wandering mind that, apparently, brings profit to none but itself by its wandering?[6]

What complicates the issue even further is that, even in practical matters, Anselm does not seem to stick to his own advice. It's not just mentally that he wanders; he is also ready (some would have said relieved) to leave his post and go into voluntary exile, though when others want to join him he insists that they shouldn't and gives all sorts of elaborate reasons for his view (V 295–97). Nor does he worry about pushing his body to the limit and exploring the outer reaches of his physical strength. *Vita* 14–15 details his excruciating bodily discipline: his fasts, his prayers, his vigils. And when Queen Matilda urges him to moderate these excesses (IV 150–52), he belittles her concerns and rapidly changes the subject (IV 153). Here, too, what is rejected and blamed in others, what in them evokes the specters of pride and disobedience, he seems to indulge in with gusto. Is the man (indeed!) playing games with us, or with himself, or what?

It will take time before we are ready to address *all* of these problems, but, going back to the mind now, we might begin by noticing that its moves, as described by Anselm, are, in fact, hardly those of a wanderer. His metaphors, when it comes to intellectual itineraries,

---

you have adopted"); and V 349–50, where he urges a nun named Mabilia not to go and visit her relatives ("My daughter, why do you need to visit some relatives of yours, when they in no way need your advice and help, and you cannot receive from them any advice or help . . . that you could not find in the cloister? . . . If they want to see you . . . let them come to you, since they are allowed to wander. . . . But you don't go to them, since you must not leave the cloister"). On the other hand, if one is really evil, the best course may be to let him go: "[I]t is not a curse on the monastery, but rather to its merit, when some run away from it because they are not looking for a better life and can in no way sustain the good behavior that is demanded of them" (V 266).

[6] Indeed, it can bring worse than no profit: it can interfere with religious life. Anselm's emotional ordeal while searching for the argument in the *Proslogion* (described in the passage quoted earlier from I 93 P89) is a good example of this interference. In the *Vita* we are told that his preoccupation with that argument "disturbed the attention with which he had to attend to matins and other divine services" (29–30). In this connection, it is interesting to note that Anselm's support of literary studies does not extend to a support of the schools; such studies are best conducted in the monastery, and must always be placed in the context of one's general (religious) purpose. See III 148 E138 and III 237 E258–59. See also note 31 of Chapter 1.

are not suggestive of the exhilarating, fearsome pleasures of getting lost in unknown territory, but rather of irresistible force, of powerlessness, of constraint. Reason is not so much an adventure as it is a jailhouse.

References to the cogent, *necessary* character of rational arguments are commonplace in Anselm. He frequently presents readers with clauses such as we find at I 21–22 M15: from two premises—(1) whatever is, is through the supreme essence, and (2) nothing else could be through the supreme essence except either by its creation or by its existence as matter—the conclusion "follows by necessity" that nothing except the supreme essence is except by its creation.[7] This fact, however, is evidence of nothing yet; "necessity" is one of those words that must be subjected to careful scrutiny, one of those traps that language throws at us and we must learn to disarm. It is said that God acts out of necessity, for example, but that is "improperly" said (see II 122 H125):

Indeed every necessity is either a compulsion or a prevention. . . . But when we say that something necessarily is or is not in God, it is not understood that there be in Him a necessity either compelling or preventing [Him], but it is signified that in all other things there is a necessity preventing them from acting and compelling them not to act against what is said of God. (II 123 H126)

It's like the previously cited case in which, from the fact that somebody *can* be vanquished, we are to infer no capacity or power of his: God's "necessity" is nothing but the natural unfolding of His essence, which nothing can impede. We may call it necessity if we so wish, but we should be aware that such improper talk is not to suggest that He is passive in any way, or prey to any limitation. Even with lesser beings than God the same qualifications are in order; those angels who refused to sin, and thereby made themselves incapable of further sin, are under no constraint, since what they did, they did themselves, and again "necessity is said improperly, where

[7] And indeed, this practice extends to his political exchanges as well. *Historia* 127 N133 describes how Anselm, during the early days of King Henry's reign, when the king was threatened by his brother Robert, once assembled all the princes and the army and proved to them, "by unassailable reasoning," that they should never betray their king.

there is neither compulsion nor prevention" (II 108 H110).[8] Therefore, to say that a rational argument proceeds with necessity is not yet to say that there is any forcing involved, any depriving of one's freedom. It could be that by this "necessary" process humans simply express their nature, their self-sufficiency (however far that extends), the incapacity of (some) *other* things to have effect on them.

It could be but it isn't, or so it seems. There is constraint here, occasionally called by its name: "But what is seen as established in the example of justice, that the understanding is compelled to feel through reasoning about all the things that are similarly said of the same supreme nature" (I 30–31 M26). And there is *in*capacity. That reason which is described as inflexibly strong at I 47 M44, as unswerving at II 110 H112, and as inexpugnable at II 185 S192 cannot be resisted, imposes itself on us, possibly against our will: "[T]he reasoning just seen can in no way be refuted," says Anselm at I 14–15 M6: we can't take it apart, we must swallow it. At I 268 D168 the student admits: "Nothing can be objected to your conclusion." And Boso, at II 85 H85: "In no way can I contradict your reasons." I can't object, I can't contradict, I can't doubt: "I couldn't, even if I wanted to" (II 86 H86).

One might pursue the active-passive strategy further here, and argue that this irresistible character is indeed a capacity *of reason* and, insofar as we are rational, of ours as well. The fact that we often experience it as a constraint, and as acting against our will, is due to the fragmentation of our nature, to the struggle fought inside us between an intellectual faculty that travels with absolute straightforwardness on its path—showing in this a true image of the Divine Word—and a thick, confusing mass of lowly drives and blind emotions—an outcome, and a symbol, of how far from grace that image of the Word has fallen. One might derive substantial help, in pursuing this strategy, from the fact that it is most often the student, the representative of the obscure turmoils of doubt, and ultimately the subterranean forces of evil, that pictures himself as chained by inflexible reason; the teacher usually moves with perfect assurance, as he exorcises one after the other all the nightmares entertained by his pupil. It is only when he speaks to himself that he lets the language of powerlessness slip through, at times; when he is made to

[8] Essentially the same point is made about humans in a passage at I 216–17 L115 that will be discussed (in a different connection) in the next section.

face his own nightmares, and cannot project them onto another. And one might even want to insist that man is *really* free when he follows the call of his nature, when he liberates himself from the fetters of animality and sin, when he lets reason guide him—the reason that no creature can oppose, and hence no creature has power *against*.

I have no objection (yet) against such claims, primarily because they are (at present) independent of my concerns. I don't care (for the moment) how such delicate words as "freedom" and "necessity" are thrown around, and where they end up falling. What I care about is the underlying machinery, the facts described by these words. Remember: I am following a suggestion that intellectual work may be more than a disengaged wheel, helplessly dissipating energy, that there may be a job this work does, one that doesn't amount to just killing one's leisure time by (sort of) chanting God's praise and assuaging one's thirst for neat and orderly arrangements.

The earlier references to Anselm's intensity suggested that we might be on the right track, and the present discussion of necessity intimates where the track might lead. There is a war fought here, over (and in) us, and reason seems to have a role in it, to be somebody's weapon. Never mind with which contestant we will eventually want to identify (if any). Before we rush to a decision on that issue, we need to know more about what is at stake. Because *there is* something at stake, apparently; it's not just a harmless game, a love song, a smiling sunset. There are humans, or maybe parts of humans, being pushed into corners, and incapacitated, and overcome, and reason has something to do with it—something so important, possibly, that one can tolerate, and even encourage, derailing precious time and energy into it, away from more immediate, pressing duties; so vital that one can repeatedly risk one's integrity in the process, repeatedly come one step shy of miracle or despair, without ever sobering up, ever learning to be safe. Because, see, you would not want a soldier to get wise in that way, not even if he has already fought a hundred battles, not if battles are not over. And so you would not want this godly soldier[9] to stop pushing his luck, if indeed what is being played here is that oldest of games, the one with lives on the line.

---

[9] By far the most extensive and detailed of Anselm's allegories is the one comparing the spiritual soldier (that is, the inner man: "Spiritualem vero militem nostrum dicimus interiorem hominem," Me98) with the temporal one. See Me97–102.

Fighting for Consistency

At I 217 L115, the student is worried about the fact that temptations are both (felt to be) able and (proven to be) unable to overcome the will, and asks for help from the teacher with the following words: "[I]f you don't reconcile the power that you prove [to exist] and this powerlessness that we feel, my spirit cannot come to a peaceful resolution of this question." At I 266–67 D166–67, the student goes further in indicating the dangers that might follow from the incapacity to reach peace of mind. This time, the problem is one of reconciling divine foreknowledge and human free will: "For though it is asserted with so much authority and it is maintained with so much utility, that in no way because of any human reason should it be doubted that divine foreknowledge and free choice are consistent with one another; however, as far as the point of view of rational consideration is concerned, they seem to be in conflict." The consequences are devastating: "Whence we see that in this question some are inclined so much in one direction that they totally abandon the other one, and die submerged by the wave of infidelity; whereas many are in danger as if holding out against contrary winds tossing hither and thither in opposite directions." So the teacher goes to work, as he does so often whether or not there is a student urging him,[10] resolves the contradiction, and brings back peace of mind. Which peace of mind, by now, looks ever less like a luxury, and ever more like an indispensable need.

The reference to the infidels in the last quote above might raise some eyebrows, since it could be taken to suggest that Anselm's rational considerations have efficacy against those enemies of the faith.[11] But didn't Barth say, and didn't I agree, that no such efficacy is possible; that we can't even expect to meaningfully *communicate*

[10] See, for example, I 22–23 M16 (What is this "nothing" from which God created everything? Is it, perhaps, something? Does this mean that God created everything from something?); I 36–37 M32–33 (How can God be in all places if those places are distinct from one another? Is God distinct from Himself?); II 147–49 Vi152–54 (How can humans be sinless at conception, and yet be conceived in sin?); II 154–55 Vi159–60 (How can Christ be a descendant of Adam and be free of the sin common to all such descendants?).

[11] On closer inspection, it becomes clear that there is no direct reference to the infidels in that quote, but rather to the danger of *the faithful* losing their faith. The significance of this distinction will emerge later; see pp. 43–44.

with the infidels, let alone win them over by arguments of any kind? To orient ourselves in the face of this challenge, it is useful to bring out one other occasion in which the teacher has gone to work to restore consistency and tranquillity.

At II 6 I11, Anselm is concerned (without any interlocutor's prompting) with the problem of how it is that, though the Father and the Holy Spirit are *the same as* the Son, they are not incarnate when the Son is, and he gives a justification for his involvement in this problem which is in the process of becoming familiar to us: "Since I feel that several people exert themselves in the same question, even if in them faith overcomes reason, which to them appears to oppose faith, it does not seem superfluous to me to dissolve the opposition." However, before he gets on to discussing the issue, he wants to address those "who with abominable temerity dare argue against something which the Christian faith confesses, because they cannot grasp it with the understanding, and with foolish pride [*insipienti superbia*] judge that what they cannot understand can in no way be, rather than acknowledging with humble wisdom that there can be many things which they cannot comprehend" (ibid.).[12] What he wants to tell them we know already, since I have already cited the continuation of this passage: They must thank God if they can understand, and bend their heads if they can't. But it is the word *insipiens* that I want to focus on here, since this is the word Barth used when offering his reasons for why Anselm's concern could not be to proselytize. "The inexplicable possibility exists that the partner in discussion is and remains an *insipiens,*" Barth said, "in which case all discussion with him is pointless and meaningless." Later we explored, and made some sense of, establishing a contact of sorts with the insipiens: that of a teacher, or even better a coach, rather than a partner in discussion. But this last quote from Anselm gives an important hint as to what the insipiens's problem might ultimately be, and if the hint is taken seriously then our notion of *insipientia* will have to come apart, and our strategies for dealing with the fool become correspondingly more complex.

There is a cognitive component to foolishness. Though the fool

---

[12] Essentially the same point (but with no reference to pride, which will turn out to be crucial here) is made at II 95 H96, where the epithet "foolish" ("insipiens") is again laid on those who claim something to be impossible (when in fact it's necessary) just because they can't understand *how* it is.

may be speaking the same language as we the wise speak, he does not mean the same thing, and possibly means nothing at all. This problem is serious, and using language in the ordinary, communicative mode will not help correct it, since it is precisely ordinary communication that fails here. But we can still try to work on it, by taking the patient, nurturing attitude described in the previous chapter; by starting at the fool's level, that is, and speaking *his* language at first, and then slowly moving, through examples and careful attention to all his faux pas, to establishing more continuity between our means of expression and his. We may be less wise than we alleged, and in any case there may be no end to this operation, which ultimately will make us wonder about its significance and about whether it really is the operation we thought it was, but at least we have a way of beginning to deal with the problem—in this cognitive dimension. There is also, however, an emotional dimension to it, which makes it more intractable—indeed, intractable period. The fool is not just an idiot, he is also *foolishly proud*.[13] He not only does not understand but despises what he does not understand, indeed laughs at it—"[W]ho, not wanting to believe what they don't understand, mock the believers," says Anselm at II 21 I23, referring to the same opponents mentioned in the last quote. And if that is his attitude, how can we ever get around to teaching him by example? We know already that no example will work unless it is received with the proper (submissive) frame of mind.

Early on, the point was made that rational arguments will not prove anything that we don't know already—that we didn't get from revelation and hold to by faith. That point was crucial in attributing to such arguments a quasi-epiphenomenal character; in suggesting, that is, that they do not substantively enrich us but only satisfy our sense of beauty and balance. Now, however, when the emotional dimension of the problem is brought out and placed side by side with the cognitive one, things get clearer. It begins to emerge more definitely why it is that, unless we believe, rational arguments can have

---

[13] Anselm, indeed, seems to believe that pride is necessarily associated with ignorance, at least of oneself, and hence that moral and intellectual failure here go necessarily hand in hand. See Me81: "But one who, after abandoning [his] pride, begins to ascend by the steps of humility, the more of those he ascends, the more self-knowledge opens up to him through the thinning of ignorance." In Chapter 3 we will see this self-knowledge acquire the characters of self-denial and self-contempt, and will puzzle over such developments.

no impact on us. "Continue what you have begun," says the student at I 256 D155, "I am prepared to understand." And unless we *are* so prepared to understand, unless we *want* to understand, unless we are committed and are rooting for the success of the rationalization and hoping to rejoice in it, nothing will work for us. Faith does not just happen to come first here, it is also logically prior—a *necessary condition* for understanding. If you share the believer's attitude, we will have enough leverage to get going on you, and possibly use what you believe already to have you come to believing more: "I will use the faith of the Greeks, and those things which they believe and confess without a doubt, as most certain arguments to prove what they do not believe" (II 177 S183). But if you are out of it, and choose to sneer at us from over the fence, there is nothing words can do to bring you to your senses.[14]

So there are good reasons why Anselm's game must be one for insiders only. Still, the infidels will have a role in it, as indeed was suggested by the earlier quote from I 266–67 D166–67 (properly construed). *They* are not going to get involved, of course, but their existence symbolizes the great impending danger to the insiders, to those who do root for, and rejoice in, the success of Anselm's efforts. They only enter the game in effigy, not in person; but it is an effigy of powerful significance. "For it is fair," Boso says at II 50 H52, "since we intend to inquire into the rationality of our faith, to bring out the objections of those who in no way want to assent to the same faith without a reason."

The struggle being fought here is an intestine one, a civil war, where the battlefield is any believer's soul. There is no question that he believes, that he wants to believe, but still he can't help feeling the challenge the infidels propose to him.[15] They suggest that his

[14] In this regard, note Anselm's reluctance to catechize the Arabs at the siege of Capua, as depicted in the *Vita* (111–12), and remember his lukewarm attitude toward the Crusades.

[15] Southern (1963, 89ff) cites Jewish criticism of the Christian faith as one of the sources of inspiration of the *Cur deus homo,* and then proceeds to explain that Anselm's arguments would be largely ineffective with the unbeliever (119–20) but less so with the believer (120–21). An interesting detail is added in Southern (1990, 198–99), which makes the whole situation more transparent (and confirms the line taken here): the problem with the Jews was not so much *their* scorn of the Christian faith (as "outcasts . . . , treated as serfs of the king, living semi-outlawed and wholly despised in areas to which they were confined," they were probably "too remote from ordinary life to be thought dangerous") but rather "*the number of reported con-*

faith is laughable, that its various tenets don't add up, that they won't stand a moment's serious examination. He is not going to be deterred, of course; he is still going to say that he *need* not understand, that his God is beyond comprehension anyway, and that faith is all that is required. But this attitude takes a lot of effort, and puts a lot of strain on him—strain under which he might collapse. So here is where the solace of rationalization comes in, where the teacher's soothing arguments will show all their beneficial effect. Things do make sense after all, at least for the time being, at least until the next problem is brought up and the next objection considered, and this will relieve the tension and keep up the juggling act that balances (scriptural and ecclesiastical) demands and (physical and psychological) resources. If faith is logically prior to understanding, understanding may well make the empirical difference between keeping faith and abandoning it.

This fight for consistency runs throughout Anselm's works. I have already cited some examples of it; more of them can be found at every corner. At I 39 M35 he asks himself: "So how will these things agree, which are so opposed according to the utterance and so necessary according to the proof?" There are things I *have to* believe, in other words (see also II 96 H97), but I am not sure I can. For, do I even know what it is to believe them, if indeed they contradict one another? Isn't believing one equivalent to *not* believing the other? At I 282 Anselm declares: "But as for what [Roscelin] says, that if he debated with me I would concede this: I don't know or believe that anybody could conclude this for me by dialectical sophisms; but I am certain that nobody could persuade me of this by rhetorical appearances." This self-assured statement, however, rests on a factual claim, and what if the claim turns out false? What if dialectical sophistry does end up forcing him to an unwanted conclusion? What if rhetorical artifice has enough power to overwhelm him? To be sure, he can make his position logically indefeasible by insisting that there is a resolution of any paradox, only one he is not aware of, at least not right now, but this logical possibility will not help if the issue is how long one can sustain oneself in enemy territory, how far one can go on willpower alone.

Often, the resolution of the tension comes by way of some careful

---

versions to Judaism" (italics mine). It is the enemy within that Christian writers are worried about, not the one without.

distinction. "For in many ways does the same thing assume contrary [predicates] under different considerations," says the teacher at I 187 Ve87, so one can begin to understand how it is that Jesus in some sense ought to have died, and in some other sense ought not to. Similarly, there are different ways in which God can be taken to be just (I 108–9 P100–101), or merciful (I 106 P98), to owe us or not owe us salvation (II 99–100 H100–102). And whenever such distinctions are made, and consistency is restored, a sigh of relief, or occasionally a cry of joy, bursts out of the worried inquirer. At I 237 D135 the student expresses mild satisfaction: "I see, and I am pleased that I see." A stronger response can be found at I 273 D174: "I very much like what you say." But at II 131 H134–35, near the end of the demonstrative bravura performance of the *Cur deus homo,* Boso's tone is definitely one of exaltation: "The world can hear nothing more reasonable, nothing sweeter, nothing more desirable. Indeed I conceive so much confidence from this, that I can no longer say with how much joy my heart exults."[16] Confidence indeed: the confidence that arises naturally from the restoration of one's integrity, from a victorious fight against the murmur of distrust,[17] the clamor of dissonance, the slander of envy.

At IV 195 Anselm writes to Pope Paschal: "I am not afraid of exile, of poverty, of torture, of death, because with God's help my heart is prepared for all these things. . . . I only ask for certainty, so as to know without any ambiguity what I should maintain by your authority." And it is precisely this greatest of dangers, this most formidable of evils, whose threatening presence is constantly evoked

---

[16] See also the other passages cited in note 7 of Chapter 1. The association between joy, confidence, and absence of contradiction comes out quite clearly at I 222 L121, where the student says: "But with this conclusion you have very much checked my exultation, since I already believed that I was certain that man always has freedom of choice. Therefore I ask that this very servitude be explicated to me, lest perhaps it seem to contradict the above-mentioned freedom." On the other hand, III 23 O123 suggests that joy may have to be frowned upon: "Shall I say what brings joy to my heart, or shall I be silent so that my mouth not be censured for its elation? But what I believe and love, why should I not confess and praise? I will say then, not priding myself but giving thanks." There is indeed (as was suggested earlier and will be further articulated below) a problem with "priding oneself" too much on one's achievements: Contentment is detrimental if it makes us feel that the struggle is over—which, of course, can never be the case.

[17] See I 35 M31: "[B]ut I feel some sort of contradiction murmuring, which forces me to investigate more diligently where and when It is."

by the fool's challenge. We need to overcome this challenge and understand, for our own sakes, not his; we don't want to be at odds with ourselves, we don't want to have our reason revolt against its own conclusions and leave us confused. Boso's exalted outburst at II 131 H134–35 is in fact best understood if one compares it with his earlier predicament. "I see that reason demands this, and that it is entirely impossible," he says at II 89 H90, and, at II 90 H91: "Again I say that reason proves what you say, and that it is impossible." And at II 91 H92, in the midst of all this confusion, when Anselm asks him whether the supreme justice can violate the canons of strict justice, Boso's laconic answer is a perfect document of despair: "I dare not think so."[18] There is nothing that I could add to flesh out my position, no detail or justification that I could offer to articulate it. All I can say is that I am afraid to believe otherwise.

THE CONSISTENCY OF WHAT?

Those following my characterization of reason's work so far may have gone through a duck-rabbit experience a few times already. One moment they are asked to think of a windy flight into carelessness, another of a tight corset only allowing for few, normalized moves, and then again of an escape route from the strictures and the embarrassments and the resulting speechlessness of a believer under siege. True, there is a battle here, and what is freedom for one party may well be incarceration for another, but still it looks as if I have been swinging too irresponsibly between necessity and possibility, and handing out conflicting messages as to where I would want the swing to come to rest. So we need to face the issue head-on now: Are Anselm's rational arguments supposed to establish that something *can* happen (that it is consistent), or that it *must* happen (that its negation is inconsistent)? Are they to provide some sort of theoretical account of the tenets of faith, or an irrevocable proof of their veridicality?[19]

---

[18] Similarly, at II 71 H71: "I dare not say so."

[19] In the end, this dilemma will indeed bring us back to the battle fought inside the believer, and to the different uses made of Anselm's arguments by the various agencies involved in that battle. But we hope to learn something in the process. (A summary of this process, and of what was learned through it, is given in note 42 below.)

Occasionally, it seems that all that is involved in Anselm's efforts is the generation of plausible views. At II 76 H76, for example, Boso asks: "What would one have to rather maintain: that angels were originally made in a perfect number or not?" Anselm's answer is, "I will say what seems to me," and Boso replies, "I can't demand more from you." After which, Anselm goes through a long account[20] of how things might have gone, received by Boso with an encouraging "The things you say seem very reasonable to me" (II 81 H81). This, however, is a special case, since the Scriptures are at best vague on the matter, and one is somewhat free to supply one's own conjectures. Most often, the case is different,[21] and so are the demands imposed on reason. For most often, the Scriptures do have a say, and the question is whether that say makes sense.

The *Cur deus homo* provides a clear insight into the nature of this operation. The Scriptures say that the Son of God, Himself God, was incarnate and killed to save humankind, and the first challenge posed by the infidels comes by asking what the fuss is all about. Could not God the merciful simply forgive Adam's sin? Or, in case that was for some reason out of the question, did not God the om-

---

[20] This chapter (which, remember, is a digression from the main theme of the *Cur deus homo*) is the longest of all the 237 that are contained in Anselm's works (some works were not divided into chapters). Apparently, he cherished the minute exploration of his purely plausible views (but see below, note 22 of Chapter 3).

[21] For a similar case, see I 270 D170. Here the question is: How could the devil, being as rational as he was and knowing that he would deserve punishment for his sin, commit it anyway? Anselm offers a bunch of possible reasons ("[I]f somebody said that [the devil] could in no way believe that God would damn His creature for his sin, [a creature] whom He had created with so much goodness—especially when there had been no previous example of justice punishing injustice, and he was certain that the number of those who had been created to enjoy God had been determined with so much wisdom that, as it had nothing superfluous, so if it were diminished it would be imperfect," and on and on), and concludes by saying: "[S]o if somebody said this, what would be unfitting in it?" To which Boso answers: "Indeed it seems to me more fitting than unfitting." See also II 65 H65, where, after going through a couple of ways in which the Father may be understood to have wanted the Son's death, Anselm says: "We can also understand . . . [it] in other ways, though these can suffice." And then there are times when he has *no* plausible views to offer. At I 244 D142 the problem is: What sort of prize did the good angels get for being faithful—other than maintaining their state? Anselm answers: "I don't see what it was; but whatever it was, it suffices to know that it was something toward which they could grow, [something] which they did not receive when they were created, so that they could attain it by their merit."

47

nipotent have all sorts of other ways of attaining the same end? What sort of a pitiful God would have to die for His own creatures? The answer to this challenge takes most of Book One and of the first nine chapters of Book Two. Through a complex, connected chain of arguments, Anselm establishes (or at least seems to; see later) that there was no other way, that it *had to* be done the way it was done. And Boso sums up the outcome quite effectively: "The way by which you lead me is so everywhere fortified by reason that I see I can't bend from it either to the right or to the left" (II 106 H107). This, however, is not the end of the work. Immediately, the two friends turn to what seems another sort of concern. Anselm raises the issue of whether Christ was required to die, given that he could not sin, and Boso jumps on it: "In this I want you to linger some. For whether it is said that he can or he cannot sin, in both [cases] does a not inconsiderable question arise for me" (II 106 H108). From this point on, the problem is not so much why God *had to* proceed the way He did, but how He *could possibly*, given what else we know about Him, proceed that way.[22]

So there are good grounds for the oscillation between necessity and possibility noted earlier, since reason seems to have *two* tasks here, at least whenever something on Scriptural record is considered: to prove it necessary *and* to prove it possible.[23] Occasionally, Anselm

---

[22] Essentially the same structure can be identified in the *Proslogion*. By chapter 5, Anselm has already proved that God is, and that He is whatever it is better to be than not to be. Most of the following twenty-one chapters are devoted to ironing out various oddities and (apparent) inconsistencies generated by the thought of this Being.

[23] For another good example of Anselm's addressing this dual purpose, see the *Epistola de incarnatione verbi*. In the first, incomplete draft (I 281–90), Anselm subjects Roscelin's position to careful critical scrutiny, deriving all sorts of heretical consequences or plain logical absurdities from it. Here the message is, clearly: Roscelin *can't* be right, so the orthodox view *must* be. The penultimate paragraph brings out this point with great emphasis: "I would have to fill a big book, if I wanted to write all the absurdities and impieties that follow, if we said that the Father and the Holy Spirit are incarnate . . . ." Then comes the last paragraph: "But perhaps [Roscelin] will say: Just as these things seem to you to follow necessarily . . . so it seems no less necessary to me, by that reasoning of mine that you yourself set forth above, that . . . either the three persons are three things, or, if they are one thing, the Father and the Holy Spirit are incarnate." At which point the manuscript breaks off. Anselm, that is, seems not to have yet developed any views concerning how Roscelin *can* be wrong (and orthodox beliefs *can* be right); all he is able to say at the moment is that this must be the case.

tries to argue for the sufficiency of the first task, claiming that what is necessary is undoubtedly possible, at least to God: "For since it is established that God must become a man, there is no doubt that He lacks neither wisdom nor power to make it happen without sin" (II 118 H120).[24] But such empty gestures don't work; the pupil wants to know more, to have more details, to hear a longer story. Unless Anselm provides him with that sort of nourishment, he will not erupt into his chant of joy. Which means, again, that two things must be established before chanting begins: that what we believe can be, *and* that it can't but be.[25]

The final draft of the work (II 3–35 I9–37) reaches the same point at II 20 I22, but then goes on to face the challenge. Roscelin's putative speech continues: "Thus show that what I say does not follow, and I will admit with you that no absurdity follows if the Son alone is incarnate, or if the three persons are one thing." Anselm's response, however, is largely unsatisfactory, as in fact could be predicted from his early summary at II 21 I24: "I will briefly show . . . first that even if there were three gods they would not at all help [Roscelin] protect the Father and the Holy Spirit from incarnation, which he thinks cannot be done without a multiplicity of gods; then that there aren't more than one god but just one. Then I will make it clear that, though the one God is three persons, however it is not necessary that if any one [of them] is incarnate the others are incarnate, too, but rather it is impossible." More (irrelevant) necessities, that is: the Father and the Holy Spirit *must* be incarnate even under Roscelin's assumptions; there *must* be only one god; it *must* be the case that only one person is incarnate. (The rhetoric of the last clause is especially revealing. Anselm makes it look as if he is proving *more* than the coherence of orthodox tenets, whereas he is just evading the issue.)

At II 30–31 I32–33 we find an appeal to God's incomprehensibility: God's persons are not to be understood as human ones, and one must be prepared to live with this negative statement ("[L]et him tolerate that there is something in God that his understanding cannot penetrate, . . . let him believe that there is something in that [supreme nature] which cannot be in these [finite ones], and let him acquiesce in Christian authority and not dispute against it"). Finally, an (Augustinean) example is offered to make this unwelcome conclusion easier to swallow. All in all, an unimpressive effort, which however, just because of its limitations, best reveals the nature of the tasks involved.

[24] See also I 273 D173: "For nobody will say that God was not able to give this knowledge to His angels in another way."

[25] An alternative way of describing the situation—and one that is compatible with Anselm's occasional suggestions that what is necessary is possible—would be the following: We must establish that what we believe must be (from which it follows that it can be), *and* show *how* it can be. That this (Kantian) formulation is not foreign to Anselm can be seen from passages like the following: "If it is so, Lord, if it is so, teach me how it is" (I 108 P100).

49

One has no sooner reached this conclusion, however, than one needs to qualify it, possibly beyond recognition. For consider now the following passage, to be found at the beginning of the same work:

> I will try . . . not so much to exhibit what you are searching for as to search with you; but on this condition on which I want everything I say to be received: That is that, if I say something that a greater authority does not confirm—though I appear to prove it by reason—, it not be received with any other certainty than that for the moment it looks that way to me, until God somehow reveals to me something better. (II 50 H51)

And that this is the understanding with which Anselm wants anything he says to be received is confirmed by a similar, indeed even clearer, cautionary statement at the beginning of the *Monologion*:

> In which however, if I say something that a greater authority does not mention: I want it to be so received that, though it be concluded as if by necessity from reasons that will appear good to me, it can't however on this account be said to be absolutely necessary, but only to look that way for the moment. (I 14 M5)[26]

Such passages suggest a novel, somewhat humbler view of the situation. Anselm will not establish, by his own lights, the necessity of scriptural claims; he will only share with his readers the ways in which they have come *now*—within the temporal, revisable dimension of human experience, that is—to *seem* necessary to him.[27] So the task here is not so vastly different than that of resolving apparent contradictions, or indeed that of speculating about the number of created angels. In this case, too, all Anselm can bring out is what appears to him, what (for the moment) he considers plausible.

But, one will say, this is making too much of a prudent man's

---

[26] See also the end of the *De conceptu virginali et de originali peccato*: "I said these things briefly about original sin according to the capacity of my understanding, not so much by way of asserting them as in the form of conjectures, until God somehow reveals [something] better to me" (II 173 Vi179).

[27] This attitude of Anselm's, indeed, extends beyond theological contexts. See I 168 G69: "[S]ince you know how much the dialecticians, in our times, debate the question you proposed, I don't want you to cling to what we said so as to hold it tenaciously if somebody were able to destroy it by better arguments and build up something different."

words of caution. *Of course,* one's conclusions are always revisable, and one's arguments open to criticism; still, it is one thing to argue for the necessity of something and quite another to argue for its possibility. The *internal logic* of the argument is different, whatever *external (skeptical) attitude* one might take to its outcome. And so it might well be—except that it doesn't much matter. There are all sorts of necessary connections established and utilized in Anselm's works, but focusing too exclusively on them, and on their difference from his occasional free "theorizing," would make us miss the forest for the trees; lose sight, that is, of the deeper analogy that exists between these projects—and of their common purpose.[28]

Return to the dialectic with (the effigy of) the infidel. He laughs at our faith, we know, and brings up all sorts of charges of absurdity against it. Some of them have the straightforward form: "How could we believe that . . . ?" For example, how could we believe that God spares some sinners and still is just? How could we believe that the Father was not incarnate if He was one with the Son? How could we believe that the good angels are meritorious, if they are not able to sin? Such claims are antinomic, and consequently meaningless. Answers to these charges are ingenious but still straightforward accounts of how it could have turned out that way without absurdity. God is just in a different sense than the one applicable to us; in one reading the good angels are able to sin and in another they are not; and so on and so forth. There are also other charges, however, that have the more complicated form: "How could we believe that it would have to happen that . . . ?" For example, how could we believe that it would have to happen that God be incarnate (since He had other ways of accomplishing His ends)? How could we believe that it would have to happen that the god-man be born of a virgin? How could we believe that it would have to happen that he let himself be killed? The absurdity invoked by charges of this second kind

[28] When this common character is appreciated, and speculative freedom is seen as the organizing feature of Anselm's rational inquiry, the significance of his logically cogent moves will appear to be this: Even within his boldest fancy, even when his imagination is at its most creative, he tries to maintain as many of his ordinary thinking practices as is feasible. He is, in other words, as creative as is absolutely necessary for the purpose at hand—and otherwise stays put. After a couple of dialectical turns, this theme will reemerge in Chapter 4 (see note 18 there, and the attending text), where Anselm's general strategy will be characterized as one of minimal revision in the face of a paradoxical object.

is not that of a logical paradox; it is suggested, rather, that such beliefs are unwarranted to the point of silliness, that they are not so much contradictory as just plain stupid.[29] So answers to them must come in the form of even more ingenious accounts to the effect that it could have turned out that things really had to go that way. Humans can do nothing to make up for their original sin—only God could—and still it is humans who *have to* do it because they are responsible for their situation, and somebody must do it or the whole creation would have been for nothing; therefore, there must be a god-man who does it. This is one way we *can* see the *necessity* of incarnation.

Admittedly, these two sorts of charges are phrased differently, and the answers to them differently structured, but the general goal is the same, as is the enemy's whose charges they are. He wants to weaken the hold faith has on us by exposing its irrationality, by poking holes in it, by labeling its content inconsistent and/or incredible, and we are doing our best to maintain that hold, to remain faith*ful*, by insisting that for all anybody knows there could well be no holes;[30] everything could be just the way we know it is—and could *have to* be that way. If we are successful, we will rebut the enemy, at least for the time being, and get a little relief from his unending threat. "My spirit can only rest on faith, unless that argument is invalidated which proves to me, contra [what you say], that evil is but something," says the student at I 247 D146, and the teacher is going to help him out and shore up his overburdened faith. For a moment, he will be free to think that his is not a pathetic castle of cards but a majestic mansion, solidly built over good foundations, ready to stand the weather and the years.[31]

---

[29] At II 48 H49 Anselm says that the infidels throw the question of the incarnation at the believers, "mocking Christian simplicity as if it were fatuous." See also II 163 Vi169: "[T]he being by which all other humans were in Adam was not false *or vain*, but true *and solid*" (italics mine).

[30] I find it suggestive to take note here of one of the (few) miracles attributed to Anselm (see *Vita* 99–100). When he reached France at the time of his first exile, a large hole was found in the ship that had just carried him across. No water had entered through it while Anselm was aboard; indeed it seems that while he was aboard nobody had found out about it (and become concerned).

[31] Southern (1990, 215) mentions a commonplace criticism of Anselm: he patched up the logical gaps in his arguments by reference to commonly accepted (but by no means logically necessary) feudal practices. Note that this criticism loses a lot of its force if one understands Anselm's goals as I do here. Then it seems much

It is the (temporarily) undisturbed relish experienced in thinking of this firm edifice that can resolve Anselm's (and my) somewhat confusing mixture of inflexibility and release metaphors when talking about reason's contribution and modus operandi. Freedom is the basic objective here. Freedom from the ghosts raised in our own mind by the irritating, importunate presence of an evil, destabilizing agency, an inimical power attempting to bring dissension and ruin into the confines of the most secretive cell, of the best hidden refuge. Fighting for such freedom requires us to be inventive and resourceful, and to come up with plausible stories that mend the tempter's constant unstitching. Often, the stories we need will have to argue for the inevitability of the existing arrangement, but even then ours will only be a liberating move; it will rid us of an insidious challenge, of a disheartening impasse.

This is the orthodox message Anselm's page seems to convey. But shall we take it at face value? Shall the teacher's and the student's own views on their wishes and feelings and likes be the final word on what this intricate performance is all about? What happens if, by an undesirable, improper dialectical twist, we take the enemy's point of view on the matter, and reconsider it therefrom? It happens that, suddenly, what is involved here begins to look quite disparate from liberation, and necessity swings back into a foundational role: the necessity, the fatality of a form of life. For what is the outcome of the operation after all? To dispel threats against authority, to shut up troubling questioners, to bring about the sort of contentedness tyrants dream of. A restless, inquisitive mind may raise doubts about the significance of revealed "truths," and you know how it can go after that: verbal puzzlement can spread into political instability, intellectual disenchantment can take us one step closer to practical revolt. Better to face the challenge on its own terms, to answer bothering words with reassuring ones, even when the bothering words have not yet been uttered, so that we are prepared for when they are. Better to be one step ahead of the opposition, and sharpen our swords through the night; dawn is near, and it might bring a new attack.

In a letter to Pope Urban written in a state of confusion and dis-

---

more reasonable that, in the course of establishing the consistency of some tenets of faith, he would point to familiar examples of similar things happening around him.

array, Anselm staggers: "Now since God's will is hidden to me and I don't know what to do, I sigh and wander about and ignore how to bring the thing to an end" (IV 83). Still his attitude is not one of defiance, or even of despair; all he wants is to be received within the comfort of the church, with all his doubts, all his uncertainty, all his ineffective deliberations. "I also beg and mentally bending my knees [*submissis mentis genibus*][32] humbly beseech your lofty and pious paternity: if ever in the middle of a shipwreck I, needing your help while storms press [on me], were to take refuge in the bosom of mother church, . . . let me find in you prompt help and relief" (ibid.). But what is true of the man Anselm is not true of everybody. Not everybody will have the same inclination to submissiveness, and how are we to deal with those who won't submit? The enforcement of power, all by itself, might have less than lasting effects; it might repress the outward manifestations of disagreement and disapproval while leaving intact the damaging potential this virus has when not addressed with the proper antibodies. While physical and social constraints are working, one might be under the impression that there is no serious danger, that the organism is alive and well, and then when the infection has passed a certain threshold it might strike us that we were indeed looking at a castle of cards, as we see it crumble from within.

An incident in the *Vita* (16–17) gives us a precious glimpse into the attitude and strategy that may be involved here. A young monk by the name of Osbern, little more than a boy, was "definitely quick of mind, and good with [his] skilled hands at various crafts." His behavior, however, was quite perverse and, on top of that, "he hated Anselm like a dog." Anselm, however, who wanted "to make [Osbern's] behavior agree with the ability of his mind," did not answer

[32] The one given in the text is the most obvious translation of this Latin phrase, but note that the phrase is interestingly ambiguous. Literally, it would mean "bending *the mind's* [*mentis* is genitive] knees" (which, of course, would give even stronger support to my present argument: When worst comes to worst, one must just let go of the mind, refuse to listen to its dangerous queries, make it comply with authority). And at least this much textual evidence can be provided for the fact that the alternate reading may have been operative in Anselm: whenever he clearly means that he is kneeling *in his mind,* he uses expressions like "mente [ablative] me prosterno" or "mente provolutus" (see IV 184, IV 188, IV 194, and V 332), which are grammatically unambiguous, instead of the more baroque (and suggestive) phrase used here.

in kind; rather, he "began with a certain saintly cleverness [*callidi-tate*][33] to captivate the boy with pious blandishments, to bear with indulgence his childish actions, to grant him many things which could be tolerated without damage to the Rule, [things] in which his age could find pleasure, and by which the unbridled spirit could be bent into mildness." Slowly but surely, the boy is tamed; Anselm extends his affection to him, shows him tenderness and care, exhorts him and instructs him.[34] When a bond is established, it is time to withdraw the privileges one after the other, time to take a firmer stand, "and if [Anselm] finds that [Osbern] has granted admittance to anything reprehensible, he avenges [it] in him quite harshly not only by words but also by blows." By now he is dealing with a stronger, stabler person, who can patiently endure reprimand and physical pain, indeed who can maintain love through all of that. By now, his battle is won.[35]

[33] In preparation for things to come, note that on the same page (*Vita* 16) Eadmer summarizes the story by talking of the effectiveness of Anselm's *deceit* (Lat.: *dolo*; Southern, incidentally, translates both this word and *calliditate* as "guile").

[34] Anselm seems to have learned of the effectiveness of this tactic in his own case, as we read in the *Vita* (172–73). As a child, he had been sent to a relative, who shut him in the house to avoid all distractions and made him study without end. When finally he was returned to his mother, the boy "had almost become insane": he was afraid of everybody and did not speak a word. After careful consideration, his mother "found a healthy resolution. She instructed all the manservants and maids of her house to let him do whatever he wanted, and [to have] nobody oppose him; on the contrary, if he were to ask anything of anybody, to do it without delay; and in this way, by the will of God, he returned to [his] previous health." The author of this passage (probably not Eadmer, possibly Boso) thinks that the experience left a permanent mark on Anselm, so that later "he strove to behave with so much discernment toward everybody, and to instruct in the proper conduct those whom he had taken on to direct, and especially the young ones, with so much gentleness, as he had once learned in his own case to fit this age." See also III 187 E189: "[N]obody should be prodded on to the path of the straight life, except who cannot be attracted to it." (Which, however, suggests that some in fact *cannot* be so attracted, and indeed it eventually dawned on Anselm that his mild manners did not always work; see *Vita* 82–83.)

[35] A generalization of this strategy is offered at Me307. Converts are there said to go through three phases: in the first one they must be blandished by a sweet, comforting attitude, and in the second faced by difficult challenges (in the third the process is complete, and its outcome must be maintained). This somewhat mechanical recipe is tempered at Me316, where more appreciation is shown for sensitivity to the particular situations: "The abbot must show to the students, depending on the circumstances, both the terrible authority of a teacher and the pious affection of a father."

Others are not so astute. As we read elsewhere in the *Vita* (37–39), when "a certain abbot" complained that, though he never ceased to beat his pupils, day or night, they remained wholly incorrigible, Anselm suggested that his methods were turning humans into beasts, and hence it was no wonder that they would show beastly behavior after an "education" of this kind. The abbot's response is quite suggestive: "'But what can we do? We force [*constringimus*] them to do well in all ways, and obtain nothing.'" *Constringere* is the verb Anselm himself used in an earlier quote (from I 30–31 M26) to indicate what reasoning is to do to the understanding, but now that verb becomes for him the object of an all-out, imaginative, emotional attack.

> "You force them? Please tell me, lord abbot, if you planted a young tree in your garden, and soon afterwards enclosed it from all sides so that it could in no way extend its branches, when you years later were to release it, what sort of tree would you get?" "Clearly a useless one, with branches crooked and entangled." "And whose fault would it be if not yours, who enclosed it excessively? Certainly you do the same with your boys."

Constraint is all right, it seems, but only gradual, gentle, *wily* constraint, the sort of prodding and pushing that keeps the stick forever out of sight, that makes you entangle yourself in your own snares, giving you a constant impression of being free to move as your moves are turned against you, as your jerks take you farther down into the quicksand.

"[Anselm] conformed his words so much to every class of men," Eadmer tells us (*Vita* 55), "that his hearers declared that nothing could be said that was more in agreement with their customs."[36] We are familiar with this mode of proceeding from the previous chapter: Fools must be met on their own ground, addressed in their

---

[36] Southern (1990) refers to the *Life of Gundulf* (Gundulf was a friend of Anselm at Bec, later bishop of Rochester) as providing evidence that "[Anselm's] talk was irresistible" (119), and then mentions the autobiography of Guibert, abbot of Nogent, who, as a young man, met Anselm and got the feeling "that [Anselm] had come with no other purpose than to talk to him" (383). See also III 244–46 E268–71, where, answering a request to this effect by a hermit named Hugh, Anselm gives him a concrete example of how he thinks "somebody illiterate and incapable of grasping higher things could be encouraged to the desire of eternal bliss."

own language, at their own level.[37] And we know from this chapter that, if there is enough goodwill in them, enough of a desire to believe, we (and they) might well succeed; in any case, no other approach holds a better promise of success. What we begin to see now, and to frown upon, is where all of this might go. You don't want to face worried, sleepless, asking minds with a diktat, don't want to make light of their concerns and questions and cries for explanation; you want to patiently answer their questions, speak to their concerns, tell them enough of a story for them to feel like all the gaps have been filled, everything has been brought back to order, the universe and its creator make wonderful sense. But is not this just a more effective tool than the rod to bring dissenters into line?

Early in the *De casu diaboli,* there is a fairly heated exchange between teacher and student on the subject of whether the fallen angels were responsible for their fall, given that (according to the student) God did not endow them with the same persevering attitude that He granted the good angels. The teacher claims that it is not so, because not giving something is not always the cause of its not being received. But the student challenges the teacher to provide an example, and when the example is given, he questions it, and when such questions are answered to his satisfaction, he still finds the explanation incomplete. As the teacher addresses the new concern and makes a forceful point, the student falters: "I see that I was not seeing what I was saying" (I 238 D136). He will regain his strength in a moment, and bring up more objections, but his phrase here is typical of what the teacher is after. What he wants to do to the student is exactly what Anselm claimed Roscelin could not do to him: persuade him thoroughly, make him think that it is not the Scriptures that make no sense but his previous way of looking at them, not the tenets of faith that are confused and ridiculous but whatever grounds he might have thought he had for doubting their truth. "I blush that I asked this,"[38] says Boso in the *Cur deus homo* (II 108 H110), and this is where we want him to be: where his attitude toward the

---

[37] See also V 260, where Anselm says to his nephew: "Don't be fond of dictating in a difficult manner, but in a plain and reasonable one."

[38] There is a lot of blushing in Anselm's works, and a lot of shame. See III 14 O108, III 18 O115, III 34 O142, III 45 O163, III 77 O221, III 102 E79, III 121 E103, III 149 E139, III 198 E204, III 254 E280, III 282 E317, IV 4, IV 44, IV 139, IV 170, and V 269. See also Me296, where the "[t]hree things that make a man live honestly among men" are said to be "shame, silence, and modesty."

infidel's voice speaking in him is one of embarrassment, where those moves that seemed so slick and fancy at first, and could confuse an untrained mind, and ultimately even distance it from "mother church," appear to him as themselves confused and childish.[39] This is the sort of victory that Pyrrhus must have missed, the victory that turns (potential) enemies into accomplices by earning their souls instead of emptily subjecting their bodies. And this victory only reason can achieve; armies and terror are not going to get it. Not the hollow, arrogant reason of those who turn away from the crowds and get lost in their own pretense, of course, but nurturing reason, affable reason, the reason that takes each and every one seriously and listens to them and speaks to them in a voice that they can understand and affectionately, smilingly, lulls them to sleep.[40]

LOGIC AND POWER

At the beginning of their book (1944), Max Horkheimer and Theodor Adorno boldly state their fundamental claim: "In the most general sense of progressive thought, the Enlightenment has always aimed at liberating men from fear and establishing their sovereignty. Yet the fully enlightened earth radiates disaster triumphant" (3). The program of the Enlightenment, consisting of "the dissolution of myths and the substitution of knowledge for fancy" (ibid.), has generated not more freedom but more servitude, not richer, fuller, better realized individual humans but subtler, more efficient and pervasive ways of enforcing social and political domination on more alienated subjects. Within the technological, clean sort of totalitarianism thus realized, where everything "naturally" falls into place and everybody is assigned his own little, specific task, there is a role for philosophy, too: "Philosophers are asked to provide a moral system containing principles and conclusions, with watertight logic and reliable applicability to every moral dilemma," and "[i]n general they have fulfilled this expectation," providing "logical reasons and evidence in support of the whole scale of values already approved by

[39] So there is indeed a point in proving the opponent to be conceptually confused (see above, p. 4); not, however, the *outside* opponent, but his representative within.

[40] Evidence that the same things must be repeated over and over again, gently and affectionately, if they are to be effective, can be found at I 224 L123 and III 145 E134.

public practice" (237). When individuals use their minds to challenge existing power structures, "[l]ogic and rationality always seem to be on the other side" (239), making the critic's position sound more and more absurd. "If you are opposed to vivisection, you should not breathe another breath which is likely to cost the life of one bacillus" (239–40); if you are repelled by the institutionalization of medicine and the ensuing consumer approach to it, you should not share in the benefits created by doctors and should leave your dear ones to die. In the end, "[l]ogic serves progress and reaction— or at all events reality" (240), the reality that admits no alternative, that denies its own historical contingency, that fancies (and imposes) itself as inevitable.

Additional articulation of this line of thought can be found in Herbert Marcuse (1964). Reason is the seat of a fundamental conflict between the subversive tendencies of negative thinking and the stabilizing ones of positive thinking. "This conflict dates back to the origins of philosophic thought itself and finds striking expression in the contrast between Plato's dialectical logic and the formal logic of the Aristotelian Organon" (124). Within dialectical logic,

> the subversive character of truth inflicts upon thought an *imperative* quality. Logic centers on judgments which are . . . imperatives—the predicative "is" implies an *"ought."* . . . The propositions which define reality affirm as true something that is *not* (immediately) the case; thus they contradict that which is the case, and they deny its truth. The affirmative judgment contains a negation which disappears in the propositional form (S is p). For example, "virtue is knowledge"; "justice is that state in which everyone performs the function for which his nature is best suited"; "the perfectly real is the perfectly knowable." . . . If these propositions are to be true, then the copula "is" states an "ought," a desideratum. It judges conditions in which virtue is *not* knowledge, in which men do *not* perform the function for which their nature best suits them. (132–33)

And of course, by passing such judgments, the propositions of dialectical logic implicitly set up a program of renovation and change— ultimately, of political change; they do not state facts "but the necessity to *bring about* [facts]" (133). Their verification "involves a *process* in fact as well as in thought: (S) [the subject of (S is p)] must *become* that which it is" (ibid.). Against this critical, prescriptive, revolutionary use of thought, the bastion is erected of a reason that becomes an instrument of power, a logic that is "the logic of domination" (123). In it, contradictions, far from being an expression of reason's essential calling to denial and reform, "are the fault of incorrect thinking" (137). So thought must be purged from them, as man proceeds "to create theoretical harmony out of actual discord" (ibid.). Formal logic, whether in its classical or contemporary form, is a way of streamlining any tensions that might surface in our experience of reality, thereby making that reality unassailable, forcing us to mentally bend our knees in front of it and turn ideas into "mere *ideals* [whose] concrete, critical content evaporates into the ethical or metaphysical atmosphere" (148).

So here is a definite proposal for the sort of job Master Anselm is doing,[41] a proposal that justifies both the emotional intensity associated with his research and his assessment of it as immensely valuable. It is a proposal that the master might have vehemently resisted, of course, but then again, it is an enemy's point of view that I am taking here. Faith is supposed to hold believers in check, to keep them humbly disposed toward a theoretical structure that is ultimately the expression, and the legitimation, of a political hierarchy. And, most often, faith will be enough, even when the believer can't quite make sense of what he believes, even when what he believes seems to go against his interests and wants; he's already invested too much in this framework to renounce it without a struggle. But *there is* a struggle, one that faith fights with the believer's own mind. That mind is ready to internalize the infidel's stance and use his obscene, sacrilegious laughter, his clever, diabolic objections, to undermine confidence, to evoke dangers and fear, and possibly to bring devastation. In doing this, mind will be acting out its nature, its polemical, judgmental character, that character which has made it possible, for the carriers of mind, to overcome many a status quo and bring about novelty and change, but that character which also makes mind formidable and hateful for any status quo. So the status quo must go to work, address the challenge, respond to it, and this it does by patiently opposing arguments to arguments, answers to questions,

[41] Southern (1990, 443–44) says: "If [Anselm] removed authority from his arguments, it was not to replace it with his own views: quite the contrary, it was to install authority so deep in the foundations that it was out of sight and beyond dispute."

solutions to problems.[42] That way, tension is relieved and the world looks fine once more: fine just as it is. It may not be all it takes to maintain stability; there may also be a need, occasionally, for torture chambers and stakes, and the secular branch of the institution will have to satisfy that. But there will be *less* of a need of this kind the more effective the theoretical branch is in allying itself with the sane, healthy part of each believer and providing it with help and reassurance, and in any case torture chambers and stakes, all by themselves, ain't gonna be enough.

[42] I find it useful to recapitulate here what we have learned in the somewhat tortuous discussion above about the modalities of this "response" by reason. First, some of reason's arguments will establish the necessity, and some the possibility, of tenets of faith, and there seems to be a need for both sorts of arguments. But second, by Anselm's own admission, proving necessity is out of his reach (and that of humans in general); at most, he can uphold *the possibility* that some things are necessary (or, maybe better, explain *how* these things can be necessary; see note 25 above). Third, considering the *role* of rational arguments in our form of life brings further confirmation to this primacy of possibility; in all cases, we are fighting a credibility gap that threatens the status quo, and hence in all cases we are to make this structure look plausible again. However, fourth, when things are seen from the point of view of the opposition, this defense of plausibility manifests itself as a constraining move; the status quo already has the overwhelming support of practice and habit, and "theoretical" objections are a (weak) move attempting to counteract that support, which is ready to kick in and maintain the conventional hold as soon as the objections are answered. So, de facto, a proof of consistency comes across as a defense of the inevitability of tradition (as indeed was intimated by the Frankfurt school texts cited above). At the end of this itinerary, the initial contrast between necessity and possibility (which concerned the logical form of arguments) has receded into the background, and another such contrast has become more crucial: that between the necessitating and the liberating functions of rationalization *in general*. Which in turn mobilizes a conflict between the opposite interests one can bring to bear upon the issue.

✣ CHAPTER 3 ✣

The Program Revisited

what wrong
Shall the bird's song cover, the green tree cover, what wrong
Shall the fresh earth cover?

IMPORTUNATE QUESTIONING

Late in the *Cur deus homo,* as Boso (in a passage already quoted) demands more detail from his friend, Anselm retorts: "I see that I cannot rid myself of your importunity" (II 117 H120). And indeed he can't, for a little further down, while acknowledging that he has no real objection to Anselm's arguments ("I cannot oppose your arguments. For I cannot in any way refute either the propositions that you assume or the consequences that you infer"), Boso insists that he is not satisfied: "But still this thing that I said always occurs to me" (II 121–22 H124). And when Anselm belittles him and his worries ("You are too strongly attached to nothing, and, as the saying goes, are looking for a knot in a bulrush"), he remains unfazed: "So bear with the fact that I inquire according to the slowness and dullness of our talents, so that you can satisfy me and [those inquiring with me] even in childish questions, as you began" (II 122 H124–25). And again, near the end of the work, Boso is happy to concede the insignificance of his queries, so long as answers are provided: "But bear with my asking something, which though you might deem it fatuous to ask . . ." (II 128 H131). Nor does he feel the need to apologize for being such a nuisance: "I am not sorry that I pressed on you importunately to do this thing" (II 126 H129).

We have developed an understanding by now of what the point of this importunate behavior might be. There is more to it, we found out, than pleasant mental and verbal gymnastics; the effect of looking into the most implausible corners—and entertaining the palest of challenges and addressing them with a whole battery of logical tools—may be that of amassing weapons for future fights and patching the fault lines of our precious island before they begin to crack. This, indeed, is just what Boso says in the continuation of one of the passages above: ". . . still I do not have ready what to answer, if it were asked of me" (II 128 H131; see also Me342 F5). And the student in the *De casu diaboli* agrees, bringing in an additional, suggestive reference to the ever-present (and ever-threatening) in-sipiens: "But don't be weary of answering briefly my fatuous ques-tion, so that I know how to answer those asking the same thing. For it is not always easy to answer wisely one who inquires foolishly [*insipienter quaerenti*]" (I 275 D175). The fool's moves may in fact be the most dangerous, just because he is a fool and unlikely to play by the same rules as we do, and hence most likely to throw us off; so we need to painstakingly practice and appropriate effective counter-moves, and be ready for when that silly voice speaks again, maybe inside of us.

Anselm's understanding and compliant attitude toward this in-sistent questioning is in line with a general disposition of his: when it comes to valuable matters and desirable goals, not only is it all right to be insistent and importunate, *you have to be that way.* One must never stop adding to one's sanctity: "Therefore, my most be-loved, always regard past things as if they were nothing, so that you don't disdain holding on to what you have achieved, and always try in an importunate manner to add something to it, even if your weak-ness were to make it impossible" (III 100 E76; see also III 165 E160). One must not be afraid to ask on behalf of the indigent and destitute: "But let anybody pass judgment on this impudence of my impor-tunity, so long as the mercy of your benignity is praised by widows and orphans and is approved by Christ, who will receive in them and will repay for them" (III 115 E95). One must not hesitate to insist for forgiveness: "With these clothes go back to His benignity: force yourself in His presence in an importunate manner. . . . Pray to Him untiringly, hold to Him inseparably" (IV 46). One must not let up providing good advice: "It belongs to you, venerable lady and dearest daughter, to suggest these things and others like them to your husband, in both an opportune and an importunate manner" (IV 160).[1] Even in his own case, Anselm is forever exhorting the soul to be importunate and bothersome in the pursuit of God and the good. "Soul cast away and thrust back, cast away when you sinned, thrust back when you implore, whither will you turn?"—he asks in his

---

[1] See also IV 214 and IV 217. For an interesting example of how this attitude transfers from Anselm to one of his advisees, see V 253.

prayer to Paul. The answer is: "Turn to importunity. They look for the sufferer to be importunate, they want the wretched to be tenacious, they love the crying never to stop" (III 39 O152). And, in his second prayer to John the Evangelist: "Soul, my soul, collect all of your passion and force yourself in His presence. . . . There repeat alternately and importunately: 'You see me, and do see me'" (III 48 O169). And, in the third meditation: "Cling [to God], cling importunately, my soul" (III 91 R144). For, ultimately, importunity is effective: "[I]f the sloth of a sleepy friend is overcome by importunity in the middle of the night, how much more will the importunity of so many years obtain from your charity?" (III 243 E266). And Anselm knows of that effectiveness firsthand. It was importunity that forced him to become an archbishop ("bishops and abbots and other primates seized me as I protested and objected, and dragged me to the church, in such a way that it might seem doubtful whether the insane were carrying the sane, or the sane the insane," IV 4),[2] and importunity that got him started on publishing his rational reflections ("Finally, however, overcome by both the modest importunity of the prayers and the not despicable honesty of their zeal, I started what they were asking, unwillingly because of the difficulty of the thing and the weakness of my talent," I 7 M3).[3]

----

[2] For Anselm's similar attitude toward the offices of prior and abbot, see *Vita* 21–22, 44–45. On the other hand, he seems to have been just as importunate himself in urging others to accept the offices to which they were appointed. At III 213 E227 Abbot Fulk reminds him of this behavior on the occasion of Anselm's election to abbot, saying: "For it's a beautiful victory to beat one with his own weapons."

[3] See also II 96 H97, where Anselm, about to plunge into Book Two of the *Cur deus homo,* says to the relentless Boso: "[Y]ou have no mercy on me." Additional references to importunate behavior occur at III 105 E82, III 155 E148, III 174 E172, III 193 E197, III 247 E272, III 252 E278, III 263 E292, and V 385. Many of them are approving, or at least tolerant; the two that are not (III 247 E272 and V 385) are also the only ones in which importunity challenges the church establishment. At V 358 we are reminded that vices are importunate, and at Me310 that appetites are; then at V 360–61 occurs a long passage concerning the importunity of evil thoughts (for which see also Me315), which I will discuss at some length in the next section. Importunity was also a political strategy of Anselm's, as one can see most clearly in his dealings with King William. *Historia* 79–87 N82–91 is the key text here, summarized by Southern (1990, 275) as follows: "To keep asking is not a very refined form of political action, but it is very wearing. Rufus was never to see Anselm again without the question being raised. In the end the reiteration became intolerable, and in October 1097 he let him go." Interestingly enough, this strategy does not seem to extend to promoting his own work: "Which work I do

So if indeed nagging works, and what it works for is valuable, nagging will be recommended; we know that the alarm clock is a nuisance in the morning, but the more of a nuisance it is, the better it will do its job of getting us out of bed and giving us a chance to stride and strive and shine and add to God's glory. One might, of course, question the value of the goal when it comes to the sort of nagging that occurs most often in Anselm's works; one might object that its progeny is, all in all, just another brick in the wall. One might side with the fool and the infidel, and loathe this astute, meticulous laboring to deprive their attack of any surprise effect, and wish the student did not bring up, and the teacher did not defuse, at least one perplexing tension, one well-dissimulated weakness. One might, to put it bluntly, expose the authoritarian flavor of this intellectual operation, and resent it, and oppose it. But for those who side with the wise and the faithful, as Anselm does, this criticism will not amount to much, indeed will not be a criticism; their tenets are, after all, exceptionless, universal, *catholic*.

It sounds clear and hygienic; honest, too. It reminds one of the way war was once fought, before history courses, in the mythical narrations of our childhood: two armies facing each other, fierce and forceful, parading their strength, standing tall, getting ready for a final hour that might or might not come but whose imminence justifies the display and the toil. Real wars, however, were hardly ever fought that way. If a straightforward confrontation came, it was, more often than not, either a desperate or a brutal move; either the hiss and the jump of a cornered cat, or the systematic exercise of superior power in obliterating a vanquished, broken enemy. In other than such limit cases, daily bellicose routine has mostly involved ambiguity, manipulation, doublespeak, and betrayal. It has involved not just not knowing who is winning, but not knowing whose side you are on; not just inflaming souls, but stealing them; not just hiding in trenches, but hiding in plain sight. Do we expect it to be any different with the war Master Anselm is fighting with the infidel? Probably not, but if we want to discover the signs of this undercover

---

not press on anybody as to be read by some [kind of] importunity, but I simply show to those who want to see [it]" (Me352). Finally, there is even room for a bit of teasing on the issue: "So in no way do I return your gift to you in order to be in any way less obnoxious to you; rather, I very willingly give you the one thing which I possess in the world and which is dearest [to me]" (III 98 E73).

operation, and the agendas of its obscure parties, we will have to look deeper than we have done so far, and not expect much direct encouragement from the official documents.[4]

The iron fist whose presence we felt under a velvet glove was never denied by anybody; the glovemakers themselves recognized it as an acceptable alternative strategy, in case the soft touch didn't work. So, as a first layer of deception was peeled away, and the image of a battle replaced that of a pleasant game, the warriors could still reconcile themselves with the outcome and think that Christ was guiding them to a glowing victory over the forces of evil. But this other mysterious struggle I am now trying to substantiate by analogy (as if that were possible) does not officially exist. It couldn't, or it wouldn't happen; revealing it is stifling it. The most we can ask for is elusive traces of it, and even after following them, and drawing a pattern in which they lead us somewhere, there will be no forcing the actors in the struggle to even admit that they are traces—signs, that is—of anything, that we are not making too much of irrelevant detail, and entertaining ourselves (truly, now!) with the pleasure of our little cleverness.

Clues

A first element that calls for reconsideration, in light of the new, combative picture sketched in the previous chapter, is the risk involved in the search for reasons. At II 69 H68, Boso, who has been the initiator of the whole process here and will work so hard to keep it on course, confesses: "In all these things, since we resolved to

---

[4] As we address the issue of the deviousness possibly hidden under the "official" Anselm, I find it suggestive to reflect on the structure of Letter 280 (IV 193–95). Ostensibly, the letter is a vehement reaction against ambiguity and "under the table" deals—and as such was quoted once before. Pope Paschal's official letter to King Henry is being disputed by the king's legates, who claim that the Pope told them in person quite a different story, one that represents his real view but that he was afraid to commit to writing. And, *in writing,* Anselm asks for a *written* statement of the Pope's will. At the end, however, he says: "As for those things which I suggest to your paternity outside of this paper, by the carriers of it, I humbly ask that you be so good as not to despise our prayers." (See also IV 228–30; V 263.) And I also find it suggestive that, of all the slandering accusations "the wicked enemy" could bring against Anselm, he should choose the one of being "a hypocrite" (*Vita* 43).

follow reason, *though you scare me a little,* I have nothing that I could object" (italics mine). And at II 90–91 H90–91, when Anselm, entirely at ease now with relentless investigation, keeps on bringing up point after puzzling point ("Listen to yet another reason why it is no less difficult that man be reconciled with God"; "But listen"; "Hear yet one more thing without which man is not reconciled justly, and one that is no less impossible"; "But listen"), he can't think of a tighter spot in which to be ("If faith did not comfort me, this alone would drive me to despair"; "You have already set forth for us so many things which we must do, that whatever you add cannot frighten me more"). A ground for such fear may be the possibility—indeed, the necessity—that no reason found by a human will be entirely adequate to the object of the search, and hence that the search itself will end up smearing with our dung the incomprehensible wonder of God's perfection: "I am afraid that, the way I am used to getting indignant with bad painters, when I see the Lord Himself being depicted with a misshapen figure, an analogous thing could happen to me, if I undertake to set down such a beautiful matter in an artless and despicable statement" (II 49 H51). But one should not be too worried on this account, let alone refuse to proceed on the basis of one's worry. The only alternative we have to dealing with divine matters in our own terms is not dealing with them at all, and such practice one certainly doesn't want to encourage. Even the actions of the incarnate Son of God we are not able to duplicate exactly—indeed, our attempts at doing so often result in the most disparate rites—but no blame follows from this variance, and no hesitation *should* follow from it:

> Indeed, as for the fact that some, when sacrificing the body and blood of the Lord, make a cross over each from the beginning of the canon, whereas others make a cross over each only when the bread or body, or the chalice or blood, are mentioned individually; but when the offering or victim is named, make a single cross over both . . . I don't see that in this the latter are more in disagreement with Christ, who blessed each individually, than are all those who don't sacrifice the chalice after a supper, as Christ did, and who call both by the single name of offering or victim, which Christ did not do. Whence we can infer that we can be different from one another in an action of this kind without blame, once the truth of the thing is preserved, since

we are different from the very author of the same sacrifice without offense. (II 240 Sa247)[5]

But there is a more serious ground for worry here, and more of a risk: our inquisitive attitude may raise dormant ghosts, and turn them into veritable scares, and ultimately work in the enemy's favor. When I first considered this danger I compared it to the threats of addictive behavior, but that was at best a provocation and could provide no resting place for our concerns. Later I indicated that such a place could perhaps be found within a context of need; bad as they are, there are risks you *have to* accept, given how much there is at stake and how much the risks can buy you. But this is only the beginning of a story, not the end of one, for now a bunch of empirical questions must be considered. Is this strategy of looking for possible objections and convincing replies ahead of time the only one available here? And, in case it is not, is it the most effective one? And, even in case it is, is its greater effectiveness worth the trouble? To sum it all up in one catchy phrase, how does insistent questioning fare in terms of a cost-benefit analysis?

At V 360–61, Anselm is addressing a group of nuns, and after some general remarks about how it is that an action is just if and only if the relevant volition is just, and a volition is just if and only if it conforms to God's will, he gets down to more practical matters, that is, to the concrete issue of how to optimize one's mental state: "But as for how to drive out of yourself an evil volition or an evil thought, understand and retain this small piece of advice which I give you." And what the "small piece of advice" amounts to is: Don't fight with those evils, because it doesn't work, but try instead to make them go away by concentrating on something else. "Don't struggle with perverse thoughts or a perverse volition; but when they trouble you, strongly occupy your mind with some useful thought

[5] After all, we don't really know why Christ did all the things he did: "But it is certain that he blessed unleavened bread; perhaps not because what was done required this, but because the supper within which it was done had this [kind] available" (II 224 A233). At II 194–96 S202–4 there is a long discussion of exactly how far one should push the analogy with human breathing in accounting for Christ's "breathing" the Holy Spirit into his disciples, near the end of which we find the following general statement: "When the Divine Scripture signifies something secret through similes of sensible things, the things that signify and those that are signified cannot be similar in all respects. For that would be identity, not resemblance."

and volition, until those [others] vanish. For a thought or a volition is never driven out of the heart, if not by another thought and another volition which does not agree with it." And note that such discordance is not to be understood as either direct contradiction, such as would result if those perverse thoughts or volitions were faced unflinchingly and answered in kind, or as the mobilization of a strong emotional response; the context makes it clear that what Anselm has in mind is a pure and simple, clever changing of the subject. Evil considerations and wishes will be chased away not by proving them evil or crying over their recurrence, and thus having them ever more present to one's mind, but by occupying the mind's territory with other *sorts* of considerations and wishes, thereby undercutting the livelihood of the former sort:

> Therefore behave toward useless thoughts and volitions in such a way that, directing yourself with total effort to useful ones, your mind disdain even remembering them or looking at them. . . . And do not grieve or be saddened concerning their disturbance, while, as I said, you despise them and give them no assent, so as not to make them come back to memory and bring their importunity [!] back to life on the occasion of [your] sadness.

And if you think this advice was only good, in a man's world such as Anselm's, for less-than-rational women (like the nuns), the bishop will disillusion you by concluding with perfect generality: "For the mind of man has this habit, that what it is pleased or saddened by, comes back to memory more often, than what it feels or thinks [to be] negligible."[6]

---

[6] A male variant of this advice can indeed be found in Letter 418 (V 363–64), where a monk by the name of Turoldus is addressed (for example) as follows: "For just as your body is segregated from the life of secular people, so should your heart be separated from worldly thoughts, and always occupied by some useful and spiritual meditation." Also, the substance of Anselm's letter to Robert's nuns is repeated at Me269–70 and addressed there to the "sweetest of sons." The theme emerging here is indeed quite commonplace in (the reports of) Anselm's sermons and conversations. At Me53 we are alerted to the fact that frequent consideration of sin can easily turn into taking pleasure from it. At Me54 the thought of wanting to abandon one's vices is considered more imperfect than either the simple contemplation of God or the meditation on virtues. At Me82 we are told that the consideration or knowledge of the sins of others "generates . . . many evils" because (among other things) it is a source of temptation. At Me121 we are invited, "as soon as [we feel the presence of] an evil [volition or thought], to resume a good

With this perceptive, expert diagnosis of a major human weakness and the consequent sensible advice for how to get around it most effectively, we return to a theme that was central in the early part of our discussion. I pointed out, in the first section of this book, that Anselm's general attitude expresses little confidence in words, and a lot more in concrete practices; it is the ways people move—specifically, the ways they *are in the habit* of moving—that make a difference, not the stories they tell. Later we lost track of this point, as first the words' potential for damage and destruction, and then the effect soothing words can have against threatening words, were brought up and monopolized our attention for a while. Now, however, around the last corner reached by our inquiry, that point surfaces again, and startles us, and makes us wonder whether we have been wasting our time; whether there isn't, that is, a much safer, quicker, more decisive strategy for dealing with the infidel's perverse and importunate insinuations. Instead of untying his knots, cut them; instead of turning the spotlight onto the details of his operation, look away; instead of trying to answer him in a manner that he can appreciate, forget him. If you do, or think about, something else, whatever you do or think about will inevitably become prominent for you, and foolish challenges to your form of life will fade into irrelevance; on the other hand, if brooding over those challenges takes an inordinate amount of your time, you cannot avoid being infected, and affected, by them.

At V 283, addressing a canon by the name of Gunther who was resisting the nomination to abbot of St. Quentin (just as he himself had done when it was his turn!), Anselm points out: "For I judge it to be more useful to you, if you preserve the quiet of contemplation in the mind through love and the obedience of brotherly charity in

---

one and focus on it, so as to expel evil through its presence." At Me165–66 a detailed, vivid sketch is given of somebody who had evil, filthy thoughts and now keeps blaming himself for it: "How wretched of me, what did I think? How miserable of me! What did I feel? What did I do? Oh what a pain! How can I be purged of so much dirt . . . ?" These self-accusations, however, do not rid him of the evil. How then should he proceed? He should forget about it: "A traveler who is bothered by a dog, if he stops and defends himself from its importunity [!], will for this reason experience a more importunate dog. If on the other hand he disregards its barking, goes by and pays no attention, soon all that assault by the dog calms down, and the traveler passes freely." And again, at Me177, the best advice against the pressure of carnal appetite is judged to be "attending to something else."

[your] work, than if you want to choose contemplation alone, de-
spising the prayers and the utility of others." Quit all that solitary,
meditative, selfish nonsense, and get down to where you are needed,
where people are requesting your concrete, practical help. For it is
the right behavior and the right example that will set people on the
right track, not the right-sounding reflections or homilies, so much
so that you can get your message across even if you don't share a
language with your audience:

> For though your holiness is placed before barbarians, whom, because
> of the difference of the languages, you can't teach by words, you still
> can't wholly excuse yourself in front of a strict judge, if you neglect
> to gain others to God. For what you can't tell them by a speech, you
> can show them by [your] life. For so much more effectively is the good
> inculcated by example than by word, as good habits are loved in some-
> one silent and eloquence is despised in someone sluggish. (III 203
> E211)[7]

There are two sides to the predicament I am in the process of
unearthing. First, words and reason may not be needed after all to
shore up our faith; proper practical exercise works at least as well,
and probably better. Second, when their superfluousness is appreciated, the damning quality of verbal and mental games receives the
boldest relief, and even their occasional contributions to reassurance
and peace of mind become suspicious; maybe those, too, are nothing
but devilish tricks, *they* are in the service of dissension and ruin, not
the other way around.

In the most important of his letters dealing with monastic life,[8]
the one addressed to the novice Lanzo, Anselm points out that the
enemy is not just strong, he is also clever ("not only is the violence
of the openly opposing enemy to be warded off, but also his cunning
to be guarded against when he appears to advise," III 145 E134).
And the way this cunning is manifested is through the operation of
a *poisonous reason* ("For often, while the malignant cannot openly slay
Christ's new soldier with the wound of bad will, he tries with ma-

---

[7] As noted by Southern (1990, 235), this was much Anselm's own situation when
he went to England: "His opportunities for preaching were of course limited by
his ignorance of the language of the people."

[8] For this judgment, see Southern's comments in *Vita* 32n. Southern also reminds us there that Anselm himself later advised a monk of Canterbury to read
this letter (V 272).

levolent cunning to destroy him, when thirsty, by the cup of poisonous reason," ibid.). To prevent the monk from concentrating on the task at hand—doing his job as best he can wherever he happens to be—this evil counselor keeps suggesting that things would be better elsewhere, or under a different master, or among a different group of people. Beware of these suggestions, for they will lead you astray, and ultimately lose you. Stick to your daily routine, follow it religiously, emphasize patience and meekness, "strive with all [of your] forces for peace of mind, without which nobody can survey the snares of the cunning enemy, or discern the most narrow paths of the virtues" (I 147 E137).[9]

But does Anselm have the proper tranquillity, when he considers and painstakingly articulates all kinds of challenges to his faith? Is he really better than a novice, is he really in control, he who says of himself: "For I am called a teacher, but I don't know that I am. I am named shepherd, but I cannot be. I am said [to be] an abbot, but I am not" (III 68 O207)? And even if he were, is it wise for him to bring up all these points for others, and paint the elusive goal of a confidence based on rationally grounding one's beliefs, when one considers that "it is always safer in things of this kind [that is, in sin] to be more afraid than confident" (IV 157), and that his own

---

[9] But note that, in the letter immediately following the one to Lanzo (III 148–49 E138–39), Anselm "praise[s] and encourage[s]" monk Arnulf's intention to leave his monastery and go "somewhere, where [he] could live according to [his] resolution" (without, however, disregarding obedience). At III 290–91 E328–29 Anselm asks bishop Gerard to relieve another monk of his responsibility for the church of Saint Wulmar, where he can no longer live in peace or be of any use. And then of course there is the issue of *Anselm's own* requests to be dismissed from office, which ranged from indirect to fully explicit. Consider indeed the following progression. At III 269–70 E300–302 (*c.* 1091), while still abbot of Bec, Anselm asks Pope Urban to relieve the bishop of Beauvais from his office; he is a good man, but too much pressed by adverse circumstances to perform well. At IV 83 (second half of 1095, two years into his own archbishopric) he reiterates the same request, in the context of a letter in which, without asking for a similar act of mercy, he elaborates at length on the misery of his own condition ("I am sorry that I am a bishop, since because of my sins I don't exercise the office of a bishop. In a humble place I seemed to be doing something; once put in a lofty one . . . I bear no fruit to myself and am of no use to anybody") and suggests that one day he might "take refuge in the bosom of mother church" (see p. 54 above). Then at IV 99–101 (beginning of 1098) he openly and eloquently asks Pope Urban to relieve him of this misery. (See also note 2 above, and the attending text.)

(allegedly) masterful state is in fact one of even greater danger and risk: "For the wiser are deceived more rarely, but when it happens, they are hurt more" (III 292 E331)?[10]

In the face of all this confusion, it is time to regroup and reevaluate, and as we do so it might be useful to become officially aware of a factor that gives the confusion some superficial structure. Most of Anselm's statements in favor of reason's value and effectiveness come from his works, whereas most of his statements to the contrary come from his letters, sermons, or conversations. When he is *doing* something he is skeptical and suspicious of arguments and questions, insistent that they can be misleading and divisive—and remember: The Holy Spirit, "as It cannot be divided, so It cannot live in discord" (III 290 E328). But there are also times when he is not (otherwise) acting, when he is (just) indulging in his favorite mental games, and then he will stress how much of a promise these games hold of final reconciliation and quiet, and not stoop to the suggestion that that promise might be a trap, that if there are—as in fact there are—better ways of dealing with hellish slander—by *not* dealing with it, that is—then it's so much safer to choose them and not even get involved with the devil's bait. "O rational nature," he says at III 261 E289, "is this a reasonable resolution, that, since there is danger everywhere, you choose to remain there, where the danger is greater"—that is, outside the monastery? But then he seems to forget that, by his own lights, rational discussion may be a more dangerous place to be than serene, operose, mindless work,

---

[10] There is no lack of negative allusions to cleverness in Anselm's works, especially when he is attacking (theoretical) enemies. Thus at II 226–27 Sa235 he quotes St. Paul while asking: "Who, I say, but one 'who is wiser than it is proper to be wise,' has so much confidence in his wisdom that . . . ?" And at II 228 Sa237 he again asks, ironically, "[W]hatever is this wisdom of the Greeks on the basis of which . . . ?" At Me360 the quote from St. Paul is given more fully: "Brothers, I tell you 'not to be wiser than it is proper to be wise, but to be wise with moderation.'" Incidentally, the concern emerging here with reason's dangerous influence has often been lost on Anselm scholars. Consider, for example, the following passage from Hopkins (1972, 53): "That Anselm comments relatively little on the relationship between sin and the intellect manifests the absence of that fear of reason's deceptiveness which haunted Augustine after his experience with Manicheism." The fear may indeed (though it's undeniably present) be less close to the surface than in other authors, but its very depth and hiddenness is an issue of paramount importance—as indeed will become clear in what follows.

and hence that, by a self-destructive loop, reason itself may denounce the irrationality of paying too much attention to itself, and expose the caviling arguer as the true, ultimate fool.[11]

Where, then, is the true Anselm to be found? In the healthy, authoritative disciplinarian who is forever preaching submissiveness and restraint, or in the lenient, curious investigator who will entertain all of your nightmares at great length—indeed, add to them? For a while, it seemed that this investigation and leniency might issue in a subtler, more decisive form of discipline, but are we still to believe that? What if, instead of giving in to the black sheep's fancies, we waited them out, and tired them out, by looking the other way? If this optional strategy works just as well (or better), then we must face the fact that our earlier resolution of the conflict was too easy, that the conflict may be more vicious than we have intimated so far, or at least more intricate. And before we proceed to thus face the facts, it might be useful to throw in one more clue—just in case the situation is not yet intricate enough.

Near the end of the first meditation (III 79 O224), Anselm exhorts himself once more to importunate behavior ("Invoke importunately the One Whom you proudly challenged") and launches an extended invocation to Jesus, which includes the following: "Jesus, Jesus, because of this name of Yours do to me according to this name of Yours. . . . For what is Jesus if not savior? So Jesus, for Your own sake be Jesus to me." Now this is puzzling, for consider: God is admittedly above and beyond human reason, and any characterization we might give of Him is only given to satisfy a need *of ours,* a need for consistency and understanding, so how is it legitimate to then use the characterization to force God into a corner, to threaten Him with being self-contradictory if He does not comply with our requests? Is this a submissive attitude, or is it rather an arrogant, and a bit belligerent, one?

More signs of such arrogance are found often in the prayers and meditations. Each of them could be dismissed, of course, and blamed on a soul too hot with devotion, but together they form a disturbing lot, especially if one remembers that these texts are not

---

[11] Southern (1963, 52) says, in connection with Anselm's habit of rarely, if ever, referring to authorities: "By nature Anselm was anything but a rebel, but in this one respect he may be accounted one." (But compare this quote with the one in note 41 of Chapter 2; the significance of this conflict will emerge shortly.)

just the ramblings of a hermit but were intended to be circulated and read, and to promote edifying thoughts and attitudes. See, for example, how John the Baptist and Jesus are called to task, at III 29 O133, to give evidence of what they talk about: "Prove to me in myself, You Your act, you your saying. Let me experience what I hear, let me feel what I believe. Jesus, good Lord, if You do what he attests, let Your work be in me. John, revealer of God, if you attest what He does, let your word be in me." Or how Jesus and John the Evangelist are asked at III 47 O167 to bear the imposition of Anselm's intrusive "love" and, again, provide needed evidence: "So suffer and forgive, if love contrives something to wrest out love. Bear with me, I say, because the love of the love of God forces me. Lord and lord, I believe, I know that you love each other, but whence will I experience this, if you don't grant me what I ask [you] for the sake of each other?" Or how God is reminded of His own mercy at III 56 O185 (see also III 83 O229): "You, I say, Who are called benign and merciful, 'exalted over malice,' are You so incensed against the repenting sinner, as to forget what You are?" Or how He is invited at III 60 O193–94 to finish up His work, after going as far as He did:

> Good Lord, you stirred and roused that [soul] in the abyss of its crimes, like one sleeping in a bed. You shook the sluggish, You urged the negligent, You made one repent of what he rejoiced in, and be pained by what delighted him. You advised [him] to ask for an intercessor, You showed him to him. Good God, You did all these things in the abyss, and do not hear one calling from the abyss? You did these things anticipating one who was running away from You, and do not look after one wanting to return to You, to complete what You have begun?[12]

---

[12] See also III 7 O94 ("Complete what you have begun"), III 14 O109 ("[W]ill your mercy be less than it's proper to you?"), III 15 O111 ("[I]t's impossible that you should forget these merits so peculiar to you, and so necessary to us. . . . [I]t's incredible that you should not pity the praying wretched"), III 16 O112 ("Let this sinner of yours prove, prove in himself that you truly are"), III 31 O137 (addressed to Peter: "For if [this sinner] has strayed, he has not denied his lord and shepherd"), III 38 O150 ("O God, who resuscitates, if God does not resuscitate?"), III 67 O206 ("I do this because of the love of your love"), and III 91 R144 ("You who make me ask, make me receive"). In connection with the passage from III 14 O109 above, Benedicta Ward has the following to say (in her introduction to the prayers and meditations): "In his need the sinner asks for Mary's intercession, and uses a reason

Indeed, it seems that the more one expects God and His saints to be benevolent, the more one will allow oneself this sort of pushing around: "Maybe I will speak out of presumption, but it is definitely your goodness that makes me audacious" (III 24 O125). For, as Anselm himself said to Lanfranc, then archbishop of Canterbury: "I will assume this concession [to be] certain, if I don't read any [explicit] prohibition" (III 131 E115).[13] And, with God being incomprehensible and all that, it is easier with Him than with any human to explain away anything that looks like a prohibition and give free rein to one's implacable needs.

The way in which I understand these passages to add to our previous worries is as follows. In the picture drawn in Chapter 2, Anselm was a dedicated soldier of Christ. If he entertained a question, an objection, a doubt, or anything of the sort, it was with the intention of answering it, resolving it, or whatever the case may be. But then it was pointed out that addressing such questions and doubts, *even with the intention of answering or resolving them,* might not be in the interest of the side Anselm was supposed to be on, because there are better ways of dealing with questions and doubts than (attempts at) answering or resolving them, and if there are then the emphasis shifts from whatever value those (attempted) answers might have in comforting our faith to the damage that can be done to the faith's very fabric by opening so many cans of worms. If this point is taken seriously, then it might seem that Anselm's practice contains an element of being on the other side—the side of the clever, importunate counselor who will be happy if we at least consider his insinuations, mull them over, and have them distract us from other,

---

that recurs in other prayers and has something *unexpected* to say about the intercession of the saints: 'If you refuse to help me, will not your mercy be less than it ought to be?' " (O61; italics mine). The pressing, irresistible character of love occasionally surfaces as an excuse in Anselm's dealings with humans, too; see for example III 252 E278, III 260 E287, and IV 18.

[13] But note Anselm's quite different attitude when he finds himself at the other end of a relation of authority: "It is true that I did not say 'I prohibit,' or 'I order you to do.' For I saw that for an understanding person it would be enough that I said incessantly: 'My heart does not want, does not approve. . . .' For the monk should not wait for the command of the mouth, if he knows the will or the resolution of his abbot" (III 283 E318; see also note 13 of Chapter 1, and the attending text). In *Vita* 77 Anselm is reported as saying that "[p]ermission deceives many," in that something may be permitted and still be a sin (see also Me75–76). Is he himself, perhaps, occasionally deceived in this matter?

more useful pursuits. And now, within the context of this perplexing gestalt switch, Anselm's occasional arrogance in the prayers and meditations makes suggestive, fearsome sense. It is as if the enemy in him—the enemy which *is* him, at times—came forth and said to God, as the enemy in fact once said: Be yourself, show me what you say to be true, prove it to me, don't ask too much of my patience. I will be bothersome, I will challenge you, I will call your cards.

One might go along with this reading, and yet not be overly impressed by it. For didn't we decide that a struggle was fought inside any believer's soul? And what does that mean if not that God and His enemy will take turns speaking in the soul? And doesn't this imply that, occasionally, the soul will be speaking with a voice that is not, indeed is opposed to, God's? So what is so special about the last few conclusions we reached?

What is special has to do with the modalities of the struggle. True, both sides are there, *in* the man Anselm, but formerly it seemed that the enemy side's main weapons were derision and contempt, and that the formidable machinery of rational inquiry was well within the walls of the Holy City: a powerful defensive means against all foolish, blasphemous attacks. Now, however, it begins to dawn on us that, if indeed the machinery is inside those walls, it might be as a Trojan horse: a means of instigating forces sympathetic to the enemy under the pretense of a beautiful construction and a generous gift. It begins to feel as if, perhaps, inflexible reason were an excuse to infuse humble believers with arrogant demands, just as (an excess of?) piety sometimes does. Pardon me, God, if I seem too demanding when I ask for some experience of You; it is my love that makes me speak that way. Pardon me if I bring up one more subtle incoherence in the picture I have of You, and follow it up in painstaking detail; it is my desire to resolve it, and rejoice in Your splendid perfection, that makes me do it.

So we are back at the ever-recurring task of this book: that of finding a sense for (Anselm's use of) rational argumentation. And we need some new tool for addressing this task, if any progress is to be made; we need some new metaphor. We tried play, and we tried war, and both of those were right to a point, but also left something out; both are too straight, not devious enough, for the sort of operation we are after. We must look at more shadowy, deceptive moves; at what does not want to be seen.

A Perfect Spy

Magnus Richard Pym is a pleaser. "Magnus of course is in whatever mood he needs to be in. . . . And Magnus obliges. Magnus always obliges. Magnus mends and fixes and carries better than a butler" (9).[14] "Magnus excused. Magnus excuses everybody. Magnus picked his way delicately between imaginary obstacles to the door, smiling and empathising and excusing" (13). When Mary wants to make love to him, he "does not resist" (15); when Aunt Bess took him to the theater, he, "brimming over with gratitude, . . . told her everything he knew in the world, and made up whatever he didn't" (88); when time came for him to go to Oxford, he "[o]nce more . . . embraced everything, loved everything, stretched every sinew to excel" (286). He likes to please: "He was the most willing child labourer in the world, so long as there was approval waiting for him round the corner" (92). Several masters at once, if possible: "Pym still has more than a quarter of a century in which to serve his two houses according to the best standards of his omnivorous loyalty" (471). And, as it turns out, he is quite successful at it. "'He's always liked,' Mary snapped" (509). His present wife likes him, and his divorced one does, too. His child likes him, as does his father. The people who run him like him, as well as those who accuse him and those he's hurt—unintentionally, of course.

Magnus Pym is an actor. He can tell funny stories "in that perfect German of his which so annoys the Embassy and surprises the Austrians," and "can also do you an Austrian accent on demand, or funnier still a Swiss one" (10–11). He manages a "gracious speech in Czech" (178), and "cobble[s] together" a "surprisingly passable Greek identity" during the course of a journey (109). He has many voices, and is "[n]ever able to resist an opportunity to portray himself on a fresh page" (221). In return for the admiration granted him by the two people who own him, he can give to each "the character he seemed to be in search of" (232). He's had a good teacher: "[H]e sat fascinated to see how swiftly Rick trimmed his manners to suit [those of the people he swindled], how naturally he slipped into the cadences and vernacular that put them most at ease" (93). From Rick

[14] Unless otherwise noted, all quotes in this section and the next are from John le Carré (1986).

he learned "to live on several planes at once. The art of it was to forget everything except the ground you stood on and the face you spoke from at that moment" (104–5). So now "'[h]e doesn't have affairs. He has lives. We're on separate planets for him. Places he can call while he floats through space'" (199).

Pym is a traitor. He's betrayed everybody who came in contact with him, and most of all the people he loved. He carved Kenneth Sefton Boyd's initials into the best wood panel in the staff lavatory, and got him flogged. He reported on Axel, and got him kicked out of the country. He married Mary for cover, and gave Peggy Wentworth the evidence she needed against his father. And, of course, he's betrayed his country for decades, and America—the America he couldn't help loving, in spite of himself—and his whole way of life. Before it's all over, he will have betrayed Axel once more, Axel who made him; he will have run and not answered messages and written the story Axel would never have wanted to see written.

It's relatively easy to say what a spy is. If party A wants to keep some information hidden from party B, a spy is somebody who will come into possession of that information and convey it to B. For the operation to be successful, it is essential that it be kept secret from A; otherwise, A will find ways of making B's knowledge ineffectual or, even worse, of using the would-be spy to misinform B. On the other hand, this secrecy does not necessarily involve deception; that is, some intentional (additional) activity designed to cover up the spy's work. Often, of course, there is deception: the spy poses as a loyal collaborator of A, or a passerby,[15] or something. But he might also simply happen to be at the right place at the right time, and gather the information and pass it on while nobody notices.[16]

Somewhat surprisingly, it's not so easy to say what a double agent is. There is a clear suggestion that deception is playing more of a

---

[15] Quite an accurate description of this activity is given by Anselm at Me48: "[A]s when somebody looks at some [others] and listens to them—[people] whom he sees in the act of conferring [with one another] and of whom he suspects something evil—and to get to know somehow what they are conferring about, he approaches them and asks whether they saw something which he pretends to have lost nearby, and meanwhile looking [and] listening he searches around them for what he's never lost."

[16] So the police won't be impressed, most often, if somebody taking (say) "sensitive" pictures insists (however sincerely) on the "innocent" nature of his intentions.

role, and that there is more of it involved, but is it just a matter of degree or is there a difference in kind between an ordinary spy and one that is a spy twice over? Consider the following statement by Kim Philby (1968):

> Some writers have recently spoken of me as a double agent, or even as a triple agent. If this is taken to mean that I was working with equal zeal for two or more sides at once, it is seriously misleading. All through my career, I have been a straight penetration agent working in the Soviet interest. The fact that I joined the British Secret Intelligence Service is neither here nor there; I regarded my SIS appointments purely in the light of cover-jobs, to be carried out sufficiently well to ensure my attaining positions in which my service to the Soviet Union would be most effective. (xvi)

Susan Laity (1987), who quotes this passage and recognizes that it "makes an important point" (139), nonetheless finds the argument "specious" (138) and ends up deciding "to use *double agent* to refer to someone employed simultaneously by two opposed secret services" (139). But she acknowledges that this is at best a working definition, that the term is ambiguous and difficult to apply within le Carré's fiction.

The reason for this difficulty must be found within our ordinary, "working" notion of personal identity. So long as we think of an I as an object among others, as a coherent, definite structure unfolding its coherent, definite destiny, there will be no room for "real" double agents. There will be deception, doubled and tripled, but when things are set straight and deception unveiled then the true pattern will emerge: what the person really is and where he is really going. At that point, indeed, you might also say that that's what he really *wants,* possibly without knowing it; personal will is not going to be less real for being derivative or unconscious. In a context like this, our man Pym is an anomaly. When he promises loyalty to Sefton Boyd right after betraying him, he "mean[s] every word" (104). When he delivers a speech during his father's campaign—the very campaign that he will eventually do his best to bring down—"he believes as usual every word he says" (316). When he watches the American dream on the circular screen at Disneyland—the dream for whose demise he is actively working—he weeps sincere tears and believes every bit of it. "And . . . believes it still" to the end of his life (499).

The most obvious way of dealing with anomalies is in terms of deviance. There is something wrong with Pym, one says; he is *self-deceived*, or schizophrenic, or a compulsive liar. He is a foreign agent all the way through, whatever *he* might say or think or feel, and is a double agent only in the "working" sense of being paid by two services. But I want to go the more difficult route of using the anomaly to make ordinary notions explode, of seeing things from the point of view of the anomaly. I want to go that route because the pattern emerging then is one that made sense to me before and has now become part of my own history.[17]

In this pattern, the I is not an object but rather the negation of any and all objects, obtained by patiently appropriating them and then playing them against one another, so that they cancel each other out. It is not a character, but a theater where many characters jockey for position, each with his own agenda, his own ambitions, his own drives. It is a crowd of spirits fighting for the possession of this one body, a mob of different readings of the body's each and every move, a rabble of conflicting and confusing predictions as to what the next move will be. Within this pattern, deception falls off as a useless concept, unless it is the deception *of the pattern,* the hiding of it under a pretense of consistency and determinateness, the ideological disarming of the I's potential for conceptual, not just empirical, subversion—the subversion of a whole way of thinking, not just of what is being thought. And "the will" is less than unseen and unknown; it is not at all, there is no such thing, and thinking that there is, that we might discover a plan under the clamoring of these voices, that the clamoring belongs to somebody, that deliberation and decision are more than the faint, inert echo of whatever voice happens to be speaking at any one time, is one more way we make it harder for ourselves to see what the clamor is all about.[18]

---

[17] See Bencivenga (1990), especially the last chapter.

[18] One fundamental feature of this model is that causal relationships are read not in terms of *imposition* (one event forcing another to come to pass) but rather in terms of *regularity* (events of one kind following events of another kind in consistent, predictable ways; see Bencivenga, 1987). And one important consequence of the regularity reading of causality is the possibility of multiple causation: there is no reason why the "spatiotemporal manifold" should not be parsed out in more than one (predictable, regular) way, and hence one and the same event made to fall into more than one of the "figures" thus drawn. With all this in mind, it is suggestive (though, I admit, hardly decisive) to turn to IV 48, where Anselm is addressing Gunhilda,

For this pattern, Magnus Richard Pym is a Platonic ideal: a perfect instance in which all traits appear in absolute transparency, untainted by the delusion of an objective (mis)construal, free to follow their own logic to an extreme and violate normal expectations in the process. The (conceptual) opposition sees Pym as a perfect spy: a freak of nature that does not belong in the same species as ourselves, a well-oiled mutation that comes without direction and without a cause, and that can be turned in any direction and in favor of any cause. But for the line of thought I resonate with, Pym is a perfect self, a perfect subject, a perfect human. He shows us what the nature of our species is, and what makes it different from all other species— that we are different from ourselves, that is. "Magnus is a great imitator, even when he doesn't know it. Really I sometimes think he is entirely put together from bits of other people, poor fellow" (427). Who speaks here is Axel, the closest thing there is in Magnus's world to a conscious, controlling will, and for Axel of course Magnus is a poor fellow. Compassion is one trick among many that you can use if your ideology is challenged by an anomalous practice, if that practice alarmingly suggests that the anomaly might be the rule, for you as much as anybody.

When Pym asks himself why he went along with the request by the Secret Service to spy on his fellow students at Oxford, he can only think of one answer: "So that the free world can sleep safely in its bed at night while the secret watchers guard [England] in their rugged care" (297). And again, as he ponders on that crucial moment in his life when he finally joined the service for good—the moment that turned out to be not so crucial after all in view of how much had happened already, but that, because of what had happened already, finally spelled out the inevitability of his sentence—the same thought surfaces: "It is the ravishment that must be done to truth, friendship and, if need be, honour in the interest of Mother England. We are the chaps who do the dirty work so that purer souls can sleep in bed at night" (455). We have heard this line before, in the context of Anselm's search: He will worry about what can bug you even before it does, even if it never does. He will take care of it, resolve

---

a nun who had been the lover of the (now deceased) Count Alan Rufus: "Though there are other causes why he died, however who will dare deny that this cause, too [that is, God's will to bring Gunhilda back into the convent], was there with the others?"

it; you may rest assured that your faith is in good hands. The worst we could say of the line at the time, we did: What if we sided with the bugging concerns? What if we wanted to leave room open for opposition and criticism? Isn't this rational sealing off of all theoretical alternatives the most deprecable form of totalitarianism? And then the data made this reading seem too simple, and our expectations not quite bad enough. As the same line surfaces again in the new context, with the new bag of metaphorical tools we have acquired, we may be ready for worse expectations and more devious readings. Because, as a matter of fact, Pym's moves are not going to make England sleep safer. "He's a searcher," says Axel of him (424), and by now we know that this search is not conducive to peace of mind.

In the beginning there was, physically, a little thin wall between Axel and Pym, and they learned to master it, to communicate through it, to spy on one another across it. When the time came for the last push away from ordinary, coherent loyalty into that other attachment for which ordinary thinking has nothing but derogatory names, Axel reminded Pym of that tiny wall, and when the push had had effect Pym agreed: "We are men of the middle ground" (407). Again, later, as his story draws to an end, "'I am a champion of the middle ground,' he tells himself, using an old phrase of Axel's" (463). The middle ground is what traditional realist modes of thought have always had the most trouble with: how a thing becomes another, how it relates to another. What is the nature of causation? When does pink turn into red? How do body and soul interact? It won't do to make the pineal gland very very small and sensitive, and the animal spirits very very fine and quick; it's still one thing influencing another, the mystery still haunts us. If we give up realism and embrace the "confused" view of the self I sketched above we will still have problems, of course, but not this one. The middle ground will be our way of life: the way in which moves that have no owner to start with get clustered together and assigned an owner for a while, only to find out later that the assignment makes no sense, that that owner is ready to be given up and the whole configuration and parsing of moves to be conceived differently. "In the beginning was the deed. Not the motive, least of all the word" (296). In the middle ground, there will be acting and suffering for no reason, because reasons are projected onto actions (logically) after the fact, and no such projection is secure, every one is a bet. Objects and their laws are shaky constructions, always at risk of collapsing against the next hurdle and being proven not to exist after all. In the middle ground, we don't know what anybody is fighting for; the best we can say is that we will find out in the end, except that there is no end.

"In the beginning was the spy" (406).

DAMNING REASON

So what is the sober story I want to tell about the man Anselm, after this colorful interlude of secrecy, love, and betrayal? Here it is, in plain English.

If we think of human actions as being such—actions, that is—because they follow a plan, implicit and unconscious as the plan may be, then we will have to say one or the other of the following things (or maybe something else of the sort): Anselm's rational inquiry is a form of entertainment, or of police work, or of subtle subversion. And, whatever we say, there will be a residue that we can't explain: this stuff is too serious to be a game, it raises too many questions to be a way of enforcing power, it's too much in earnest to be the devil's work, however indirectly. If, on the other hand, following Anselm's (occasional) explicit advice,[19] we don't think of actions that way, we don't assume that they receive their dignity from the-

---

[19] In addition to passages already quoted, consider Me88 ("For mostly man speaks more with action than with words"). Occasionally, Anselm stresses the importance of intention for the proper interpretation of an action. Thus at Me101 intention is said to resemble the head of Christ's soldier ("[J]ust as the head presides over all other parts of the body, so intention seems to preside over all other tools of the inner man"; see also Me150), and at II 226 A235 what makes the difference between the Christians and the Jews is the intention with which a specific rite is performed. But other passages suggest that "intention" may be just shorthand for how a specific move fits into the general context of one's behavior. Thus at Me89–90 Anselm says that one is not to be called virtuous or vicious on the basis of individual actions, but only when such behavior has become a habit. At Me79 we are told that outer virtue is of no value without inner virtue, but the example given to illustrate the point is an interesting one: "For when one is seen [to be] intent on fasting, but [also] easily angered, if he were to be praised by somebody on account of [his] fasting, immediately another will answer: 'Who cares about his fasting,' he will say, 'when he gets so inflamed about nothing?'" So the practice of deciding on one's "inner" virtue bypasses declarations of intention altogether, and reduces to comparing instances of one's *outer* behavior.

ory and talk but insist instead on their materiality, on their practical way of taking care of themselves and getting established by sheer repetition and infecting even those with whom we share no language and can therefore share no explanation, no argument, and no story . . . well, if we switch to that other conceptual mode, then there is no reason for us to choose *one* owner for Anselm's moves. He is a man of the middle ground, like all of us in a way but also more than most of us, because more than most of us he is pushing his search to the outer limits, taking roads that are most often blocked, uttering words that are not often heard.

More than once in his works and conversations, Anselm compares the good man with a cubic stone: a stable object with six equal sides "that sits firmly where it fell on whatever side [it fell on]" (Me146; see also Me195, Me305, and Me314). And he also tells us that, however good it is to make peace between two others, or between oneself and another, "more subtle" and "more difficult" than either of those, but also "so much more pleasing in the eyes of God" is the peace one makes with oneself, between one's spirit and one's appetites (Me157). The image suggested by these remarks is that of a man perfectly self-centered, entirely at ease with himself, untroubled by circumstances, led by the firm grip of his reason to give each aspect of his life its proper due. But how is Anselm to attain this ideal? Consider his description of monastic discipline at Me68:

[T]he hardship of the Rule forces [one] to stay awake when he would like to sleep, to starve when he would like to eat, to stay thirsty when he would like to drink, to remain silent when he would like to speak, to read and sing when he would like to rest, to sit when he would like to stand or walk, or to stand or walk when he would like to sit, to sustain many blows, to entirely abandon his own will.

Is this a way of making somebody stronger and stabler, or a way of breaking him? To be sure, after enough incarceration and torments, after screaming that he wants out and even threatening to kill those who hold him, the finally tamed novice will thank the very people he threatened and feel himself relieved and cured (Me70–71), but does this mean that the ordeal is over? Not when we are told that "the essence of a monk is to rejoice that his being is not his own, for the sake of God" (reported by Elmer, prior of Canterbury from 1128 to 1137, quoted by Southern, 1963, 272; see also Me161). Not when propria voluntas is *defined* to be *disobedient* will, a will that strays from God's command (Me40, Me309). Not when humility, taken all the way to self-denial and self-contempt,[20] all the way to enjoying being victimized (Me110–13), is called the "firm foundation" of all virtues (Me80). Here the emphasis is as far as it could be from the balanced, steady image of the cubic stone, its center of gravity well inside itself, resilient and robust, unmovable and unworried. The emphasis is on questioning one's every move, on looking for what is wrong with it, on *presuming* it wrong, on calling on everybody's collaboration to find out what is wrong with it—and to administer the proper punishment.

It will be said that playing with one's balance is a way of fortifying it; that higher resistance and strength can be acquired by challenging, excruciating exercises. This is well and good, but what if *all you ever do* is challenge and excruciate yourself? What if by breaking your integrity, by starving and beating and humiliating yourself, you make appetites speak that had never before—and would never have otherwise—surfaced? Didn't we say that the best way to deal with appetites is to leave them alone? That we shouldn't even consider other people's sins so as not to get infected by that very thought?[21] Why, then, such an obsessive concern with *one's own* sins, such an urge to uncover them, to painstakingly (and painfully) articulate their horror?

It will be said that you are preparing yourself for another life, one in which you will indeed be a solid, firm, cubic cornerstone, a content and quiet and impassible soul. And, again, this is well and good. But what is your practice right now? Consider the fact that, in order to get to your destination, you must do, and keep on doing until the end, quite the opposite of what you will be doing there—that, to finally become a good man, you have to behave as if you weren't. For a moment, don't look at the transcendent reality (or is it a fic-

[20] See III 29 O133: "I hate what is from me." Southern (1990) insists on the extreme character of Anselm's self-denial. His most explicit statements come from a section significantly entitled "Anselm no humanist," where we read that "introspection is simply the beginning of the road to self-contempt, and only accidentally a journey of self-discovery" (449), and that "[a]s often in Anselm, one might think that there is an element of mental sickness in this love of contempt" (450).

[21] See the passage from Me82 quoted in note 6 above. As additional evidence of the existence of a conflict, however, Anselm suggests at III 14 O108–9 that what may be worse than the "detestable" character of manifest sins is how "incurable" they are when hidden.

tion?) that gives your life its extrinsic justification.[22] Look at the middle ground where you are *now* glued.[23]

At I 113–14 P105 in the *Proslogion,* Anselm has already established that God exists and is omnipotent, eternal, merciful, and just. But he can't rejoice as he had expected: "And here again is confusion, here again grief and sorrow meet one looking for joy and delight! My soul was already hoping for satiety, and here again it is overwhelmed by want!" A new problem has to be considered, a new source of puzzlement and fright: How can God, who has no parts, be at different times? The familiar reference to His incomprehensibility is uttered: "These are many things, my narrow understanding cannot see so many together with one view, to rejoice in all of them together." But, as usual, Anselm is not satisfied with acknowledging this limitation, and proceeds to find a way in which the problem can be solved and God be made more accessible. Nothing out of the ordinary, except for a peculiar phrase he uses while still expressing his despair: "[W]hen we want to search we don't know [how to], when we search we don't find, when we find it's not what we are searching for." In the view I am recommending now, these words are to be taken literally and understood as a powerful summary of the whole Anselmian itinerary—indeed, of rational search in general.

Away from the middle ground, from where the clamor is loudest and most confused, and from the pushing and shoving and pressing

[22] Not just your personal life, in Anselm's view, but that of all humankind. Anselm seems to think that the only point of human history is that of reaching that perfect number of good souls that God established from the beginning were needed for His City—after which, probably, this history will come to an abrupt end. (See, for example, the *Cur deus homo,* Book One, chapter XVIII, already cited on p. 47 above. Note how the present considerations allow us to make more sense of this chapter's [comparatively] enormous length. It is a digression from the main theme of the work, to be sure, but in no way is *its* theme marginal to Anselm's interests.) Within such a view, it doesn't even make sense to do political work to improve on existing institutions; indeed (who knows?), *evil* institutions might be an occasion for bringing about more martyrs and saints.

[23] This concentration on one's practice is an obvious way of articulating the general worry expressed at the end of Chapter 1 about the significance of trying to reach the unreachable. What is transcendent cannot by definition be attained, so if one becomes suspicious about using a reference to it in characterizing a given form of life, one is naturally led (as, indeed, was suggested in Chapter 1) to focus on the actual unfolding of that form of life.

that makes for that loudness and confusion, the misleading picture of cubic, consistent selves—objects among others—is relatively harmless. A consistent set of moves does take hold of most of us, after all, and makes it easier to say what or who we are, what we want and where we are going. It's just a fact that this happens, of course, an empirical matter, but given how widespread it is one is naturally led to think of it as a conceptual necessity, and to end up with a reassuringly simple, infectiously optimistic picture of human dealings. But in the middle ground, this nice picture won't work, and if we are past bringing violence to bear upon the issue, theoretical or practical—if we are past calling difference insanity or attempting to destroy it, that is—then we will have to admit that often what is found is not what was searched after, not (only) because an empirical mistake was made, but because it is a conceptual mistake to describe what was happening as searching after anything.

Chapter VII of the *De casu diaboli* belongs to the student. His latest concern has just been answered, but he's not satisfied and is about to issue yet another elaborate question. As he does this, he expresses frustration: "But I don't know why it is, that when I hope I am already reaching the end of the inquiry, then even more I see other [questions] arise as if sprouting out [*pullulantes*] of the roots of the questions that were cut down" (I 244 D143). Once again, the theme of importunity surfaces here; it will never end, never leave me alone, I cannot bring the search to a close. But the interesting variant this passage introduces is that no*body* is playing the role of the importunate questioner. The questioning has acquired a life of its own, and continues to use up human bodies and resources, blind to their needs, uncaring of their pain and fear, obtuse, ruthless, invincible.

Reason was born negative, Marcuse advises us; its calling was antagonistic to reality, its point was to establish that what is cannot be true. Then, along the way, sly tactics were found to turn this explosive device into a household appliance, to subvert its subversiveness; reason was used against itself, and in favor of the great worldly powers, its official goal became one of proving that what is real is rational. I agree with this reconstruction, and with its emotional tone; I, too, despise logic as an instrument of domination, as a parasite eating the little leftovers between the shark's teeth and keeping them clean and shiny. I, too, am embarrassed and indignant when yet another repentant trickster articulates yet another obscene proof that the system is optimal and supremely efficient and necessarily real. But then I find consolation—or maybe I should say, so does subversive reason *in me*—in the thought that it's not so easy to play with fire.

You may well have started importunate questioning with the idea (or under the delusion) that you could turn it to a conservative use, that you could resolve once and for all the system's eventual problems and make it stand forever and ever, unassailable and firm. But practices have a way of mocking our principles, scrapping our predictions, thrashing our confidence. And the practice of questioning the system *in order to establish it* is, after all, a practice *of questioning the system,* and if that is what you do, you will end up *in fact* working for a different master than you thought. For the enemy, that is; the snaky, viscid deceiver who wants you to look into things and search for the knowledge of good and evil. He knows that it's enough if you get started; then the process will take over, and you will be damned. You will be looking for a proof that cleans Euclid *ab omni naevo* and will discover a credible, coherent alternative to the space you were born in. You will be attempting a final vindication of ordinary beliefs and will generate one aporia after another and wake up sleepy souls and initiate centuries of challenging, provocative inquiry. You will be struggling to provide the believer with an answer for every question, a resolution of every paradox, and will uncover more paradoxes than were ever conceived and have the sky pullulate with their menacing presence.[24] You will be a spy, in sum; a double agent conducting a silent war against those who think they are running you, against that agenda of theirs that you have swallowed. And of course your moves will sometimes favor your masters and be used to build safer, more comfortable cells, and of course you will think that that's their point and will glow when the point is reached, if

[24] Some specific examples of this infectious process may be in order here. At I 187 Ve88 the teacher uses a distinction concerning "justly beating somebody" to shore up his position, and at II 57 H56–57 *the same* distinction is used by Boso to attack the consistency of faith. At II 31 I33 the Augustinean example of the spring, river, and lake is cited to make the Trinity less ineffable, and at II 203 S211 *the same* example creates problems for the claim that the Holy Spirit proceeds from both Father and Son. At II 123 H126 (quoted on p. 37 above) the equation between necessity and either compulsion or prevention is brought out to defuse the suggestion that God ever be necessitated to act, and at II 246–47 C182–83 *the same* equation is used to argue that, when I sin willingly, I am compelled to will to sin (and, when I don't sin, I am prevented from willing to sin).

only for a brief, tantalizing moment. This is the rule in the middle ground, where moves circle in space waiting for a driver, for a fiction telling them what moves they are, of what family they are the offspring. Just as naturally, your subversive (sub)persona will come up for air, now and then, and will vent barely veiled irritation at the boss; ask Him to do His part, to come out and be seen, to take some of the burden. Such occasional lapses of faith will not affect your ordinary loyalty. You will quickly come back to your senses, realize that you have been out of control, bring up your avid love as an excuse. And you will go back to the middle ground where you belong, to your duplicitous reconnaissance of the system's delicate structure, to your maddening concern for the oh-so-many ways in which that structure could break. [25]

A final, fatuous note. Like all spies, Pym and Anselm had more than one name. [26] As it turns out, they shared their last one. "'Canterbury. The name is Canterbury,' he heard himself say as, the fuse safely mended, he pressed a deposit on her. A city had found a home" (18).

[25] Once again, as I strive to articulate such an unorthodox reading of Anselm's moves, I find it useful to turn to Richard Southern, this finest, most sensitive, and most comprehensive of contemporary Anselm scholars. "In the contrast between the austerity of his life and the emotional warmth of his friendships, between the rigour of his Prayers and the mildness of his disposition, between the eremitical strain in his own piety and his acceptance of the increasing wealth of ornament in his cathedral church, this most uncompromising of men stands where extremes meet, and embraces both" (1990, 328). "The ambiguities in the whole development [of the relations between Anselm and Eadmer] illustrate one of the permanent features of Anselm's influence: although he was the most lucid and decisive of writers, and knew exactly what he meant, he cast over every subject an iridescence filled with contradictory possibilities" (ibid., 436). For Southern the historian, such judgments are a point of arrival; for me, as a philosopher, they are the beginning of a quest for explanation—to be pursued wherever it might lead.

[26] To this day, Anselm is known as Anselmo d'Aosta in Italy, where he was born, and as Anselm of Canterbury virtually everywhere else.

✣ CHAPTER 4 ✣

That, Than Which a Greater
Cannot Be Thought

The impossible is still temptation.
The impossible, the undesirable,
Voices under sleep, waking a dead world,
So that the mind may not be whole in the present.

UPPER BOUNDS

SNOW WHITE committed suicide on June 7, 1954, apparently by
dipping an apple into a solution of potassium cyanide and then taking several juicy bites off it. No prince revived her. The inquest was
brief, and silence fell quickly.

Snow White was Alan Turing, a logician and onetime spy, who
all but won the Second World War for England by breaking the German naval code. But that time was gone, and Turing (no umlaut,
please!)[1] had worn out his welcome. Right then, he was just an
annoyance.

In a way, he had been one all along. Very much a loner, he couldn't
communicate effectively with other people, and, when he had to, his
need for rigor and truth translated into a curious, awkward, irritating literalness that made him look a lot like one of his own machines—as "when his identity card was found unsigned, on the
grounds that he had been told not to write anything on it" (232).[2]

---

[1] Andrew Hodges's text (1983), referred to through the early part of this section,
quotes the following entry from the glossary of the 1953 book *Faster than Thought*:
"*Türing Machine*. In 1936 Dr Turing wrote a paper on the design and limitations
of computing machines. For this reason they are sometimes known by his name.
The umlaut is an unearned and undesirable addition, due, presumably, to an impression that anything so incomprehensible must be Teutonic" (479). Quite an irony
for a man who had done as much as anybody to defeat the Germans! But then, irony
is what the present book is all about.

[2] Southern (1963, 6) finds "a certain unquestioning literalness of outlook" to
characterize "the direction of [Anselm's] whole life . . . in old age as . . . in childhood." See also ibid., 155: "Anselm fought like a somnambulist whose blows were
difficult to counter because they were impossible to predict."

Not even in the academic environment where he spent most of his life was he comfortably at home—or was it the environment that was not at home with him, what with his insistence on thinking and seeing for himself (79), his skepticism (87), and his tendency to rediscover whatever technical tools he needed instead of checking "the literature"; what with his anti-intellectualism (69), his desire to turn technocrats into ordinary people (364), and his practical efforts to make them obsolete by mixing instructions with data and thereby giving a universal computer the key to our future. And, of course, he was a homosexual, "in a society doing its best to crush homosexuality out of existence" (129), a "traitor to masculine supremacy" (74) forced to lead a double life and to be selective about whom to tell, forced to be officially invisible, as it were.

There had been something else invisible in the early 1940s, the German U-boat, and as long as it remained invisible one could develop no strategy against it. As an essential premise to defusing this weapon, one needed to penetrate the enemy's mind—its whole communication system, its logic—and Turing was "a natural recruit" for this sort of enterprise (148). A successful one, too, for eventually the German Enigma machine gave way ("by the end of 1943 the British had a clearer idea of where [the U-boats] were than did their own command," 263), Allied ship sinkings decreased dramatically, and the battle of the Atlantic was won.

During that fated period of world history, anything could happen. With Churchill backing him all the way, Alan Turing the social misfit found himself at the very center of things, able to make the authorities comply with his requests, to redirect fleets and troops, to deal with the Americans single-handedly. The war opened an "immensely wider horizon" to science (252) and allowed for gambles that would otherwise have been unthinkable; it "[broke] down the barrier between theory and practice" (307), between rarefied intellectual concerns and the most concrete matters of life and death.

But it didn't last. It couldn't. If indeed "[i]ntelligence had won the war" (362), then those "magic machines, incomprehensible to military men and administrators" (499) that had done the trick could also lose the next war, and the whole system with it. "Success and danger were opposite sides of the same coin" (ibid.). "The war had given [Turing] a false sense of what was possible" (376): at that time, a direct appeal to the Prime Minister would work wonders. But "by 1947 the war might as well have never been" (368): barriers were coming back in a hurry, ambitious plans were sidelined within the general inertia, and Turing, who had a knack for "producing ideas which fell into no neat compartment of thought" (447), found "[h]is very existence [to be] a glaring embarrassment" (508). His "iconoclastic 'originality' had been acceptable in the brief period of 'creative anarchy,' which had even stomached the arrogance and will-power required to solve the unsolvable Enigma, and force the implications upon an unwilling system" (509). But now "a very different mentality prevailed" (ibid.), and for that mentality Turing was a loose cannon: a man filled with lots of sensitive, "classified" information, given to the unpredictable turnabouts of genius, and vulnerable to sexual blackmail. In a country that was beginning to discover its real-life Magnus Pyms (Burgess and Maclean disappeared on May 25, 1951), such guns had to be unloaded—and buried, if possible.

So normality came back with a vengeance. Not only was Turing's war work unmentionable, even his pioneering contributions to the development of the computer went into hiding. "Already by 1950, Alan Turing was an unperson, the Trotsky of the computer revolution" (408). For a year, between April 1952 and April 1953, he was subjected to a hormone treatment to "cure" him of his "disease." When a Norwegian (male) friend came to visit him in March 1953, immigration officials sent him back and the two never met. Suicide was only the next step in this logical progression, and Turing the logician and patriot could not fail to see the necessity of it.

At the crossroads where we are in our journey, this disturbing episode acquires the status of a telling morality play. Rational inquiry, we decided, is several things at once; the servant of several masters, the playing out of several plans. It is an entertaining, possibly addictive game of skill, *and* it is a formidable piece of machinery that can terrorize, disconcert, and rout all enemies, real and potential, of the status quo, *and* it is a subtle destructuring device, able to infuse the populace with dangerous, evil questions and doubts. When a new logical twist is evidenced, a new possibility uncovered, a new threat to coherence formulated, somebody in me will rejoice in the new intellectual challenge, somebody else will experience a (moral?) thrust to put everything back in order, and yet somebody else will smile with devilish scorn at the king just found with his pants down. Then all of these agents will go to work, doing essentially the same thing—articulating the insight, fleshing it out, detailing the world intimated by it, proving this world to be *really* possible (or impossible). Because their practice is essentially the same, their struggle will be one of narratives: a struggle among different ways of recounting the same vicissitudes, with different emphases and, hopefully, different endings (hopefully for the tellers, that is). If a winner emerges in this struggle—and then it's only a temporary winner—his prize will be exiling the enemies underground, concealing them, appropriating the (official) communication lines. It will not be killing them outright, or even inhibiting their moves. It will not because it *cannot*: it is one and the same activity that fits all these different descriptions, works for all these different purposes, incarnates all these different souls. It is one and the same painstaking logical investigation that both opens sundry cans of worms and aspires to seal them forever, that invades with merciless light the most remote corners of the most faraway closets and reveals the existence of the most frightening skeletons, while proceeding in earnest to perform the ultimate spring cleaning—and enjoying every minute of this strenuous exercise.

In general, narrative victory is not enough for the powers that be. The activity itself must be countered, not just its description. There are times when the payoff is worth the risk, of course: if the system is under severe stress, and on the verge of collapse, it will encourage any sort of experiment, use any sort of help, possibly under some edifying cover. But then those times are past, and in the normal course of events moderation will be the rule: if potentially disrespectful inquiring is to be allowed at all, caution will have to be exercised. External boundaries will be imposed on it, boundaries on *where* inquiries can be performed, or *when,* or *by whom.*[3] It will be decided, say, that only people who have already dedicated their lives to the system and have gone through a long, demanding sort of training can be let play the game: "[L]et nobody immerse himself temerariously in the thickness of divine questions, unless first he has acquired seriousness of habits and wisdom within the firmness of faith, lest by wandering with irresponsible levity through the many diversions of sophisms, he be trapped by some tenacious falsehood"

[3] These external boundaries are discussed in chapter 6 of Bencivenga (1990), where the additional point is made that they are not necessarily external in a psychological sense: they can well be (and often are) internalized by the players. They are external in a logical sense: they do not follow from a definition of the game the players take themselves to be playing.

(II 9 I13; see also I 284–85). "'[J]ust as weak and strong bodies have each their own [kind of] food according to their quality, so do weak and strong souls have each their own [kind of] food according to their capacity'" (*Vita* 39), hence some souls will have to be fed just like children are, never being handed a whole fruit but rather receiving small pieces (Me274).[4] Also, play will only be made possible within enclosed areas, sanctuaries that are physically separated from the houses and markets and fields where ordinary people conduct their ordinary activities.[5] And again, even in their sanctuaries the dedicated ministers of the system will not be allowed to inquire into *everything*; some issues will be beyond their scope, some words will be unquestionable, some truths will be matters of experience (of revelation, for example), adhered to by faith, and never addressed—not to mention challenged—by rational reflection.

But the presence and effectiveness of such external boundaries must not blind us to the fact that there may be limits emerging from the outcome of the narrative struggle, too, ways in which whatever story happens to gain the upper hand might define the activity so as to make some moves not just forbidden but impossible. Which is just as well, since no external boundary is insurmountable, and hence none is safe. We know how importunate logical investigations can get, how far they can spread, how much pressure they can put on the most fundamental beliefs, on the strictest authorities.

Once again, Alan Turing is a symbol of what I am talking about. True, he was a freethinker, a relentless inquirer, a dangerous experimenter with things previously unheard of and unknown, and he did have to experience, partly as a consequence of this danger he represented, a number of hurtful restrictions on his personal liberty. But he was also the person who, in his classic text (1937), established fundamental boundaries on what effective computability can achieve, not by bringing (external) power to bear upon the issue but by a simple working out of the (internal) logic of effective computability itself. So whatever *other* (subversive? authoritarian?) games Turing might have been playing, and whatever limits might have been imposed on such games by a suspicious system, there were

---

[4] See III 138–39 E124–26, where Archbishop Lanfranc bitterly complains to both Anselm and his own nephew and namesake because the latter contravened his explicit order not to read for a whole year after entering the monastery—not until, that is, "he had knowledge of the psalms and some familiarity with his order."

[5] See note 5 of Chapter 2, and the attending text.

limits to the game he believed himself to be playing, limits that followed from the very definition of that game. As it turns out, much the same was true for Anselm. There were internal boundary conditions on his game, too—*upper* boundary conditions, to be precise.

Anselm characterizes his task as that of understanding what he believes. This is the narrative that takes hold of his consciousness, the tale that he is going to tell about what he is doing. On the other hand, we know from Chapter 1 that what he believes cannot be understood: A finite mind cannot decipher the mystery of God's essence and activity. "Therefore who will pretend to even think that the human understanding could penetrate how wisely, how wonderfully so inscrutable work was done?" (II 117 H119). God is incomprehensible, inconceivable, ineffable, and hence the project of comprehending Him, conceiving Him, and articulating our conception and comprehension in words will necessarily fail, not (just) because of poor execution on Anselm's (or anybody's) part but for intrinsic and essential reasons. It was precisely this point that made us wonder whether perhaps Anselm was to achieve something else through his efforts, given that the goal the efforts were ostensibly aiming at was not within reach. And we have found a couple of things that he might have been getting while searching for his unattainable God. Now, however, the suggestion surfaces that the very unreachability of the goal and the very unattainability of God may be playing a crucial role here, that they, too, may be weapons in the war fought by the mysterious masters of Anselm's moves.

God is defined as the upper bound of conceivability, by an essential use of negation. If God's concept were generated by adding up features, one could always wonder whether more features might be added, and a higher sort of perfection delineated. But God is that, than which it's *not* possible to think of anything greater. Such is His entire essence; whatever else He is, it must follow from this clause. Lots of negative things follow: He can*not* (be conceived to) have a beginning or an end, or be limited by any place, or be deficient in any way.[6] And, of course, one important positive matter also ap-

---

[6] For a particularly strong statement of such impossibilities, see I 33 M28: "[L]et [anyone] who can [do it] think of when this thing began to be true or was not true, that is, that something was going to be; or when this thing will cease to be true and will not be true, that is, that something was past. For if neither of these can be thought . . . it is impossible to even think that truth has either beginning or end."

pears to be settled: This highest of conceptions must be realized. God must be. The inference on which this conclusion is based is probably delusive, and later I will try to uncover the structure of the delusion.[7] Here my concern is different: I am interested in what the conclusion does for Anselm, in how it fits his general scheme of things.

Anselm walks a thin line when trying to pull off his celebrated argument. On the one hand, because of his negative characterization of God, he can only require a bare minimum in terms of what God's conceivability amounts to. Under pressure, we have seen him reduce it to the pure and simple uttering of certain words in a language with which one is familiar. I can "think of" *ineffable* because I can use the *word* "ineffable," and I can "think of" *unthinkable* because I can use that word, too. On the other hand, what he is (allegedly) after is reaching (a better) understanding of his faith, so parroting words will not be enough; the *sense* of those words must be somehow accessible, too, at least at the end of the argument. By then, one must have *understood* that God exists, not just said it. And there is plenty of room between the Scylla of this necessity and the Charybdis of the earlier incomprehensibility for the arguer to fall and crash. Now, however, my question is: What if he did *not* fall, and did realize a substantial amount of cognitive fulfillment by utilizing those sparse conceptual resources?

Chapter XV of the *Proslogion* comes after God's existence and some of His attributes have been proved, and consists of the following revealing passage: "Therefore, Lord, not only are You [that] than which a greater cannot be thought, but You are [also] something greater than can be thought. For since something of this kind can be thought: if You are not that very thing, something greater than You can be thought; which cannot be" (I 112 P104). There is a suggestive resemblance between this passage and contemporary diagonal arguments for impossibility results (nondenumerability, undecidability, and the like): I can think that there is something greater than anything I can think of, hence that, than which I can think of nothing greater, must be such that I can't think of it.[8] And, of

---

[7] See Appendix 1 below.

[8] See also V 395: "When I want to write to your highness, I can't find any words by which I could express [my] affection . . . ; unless perhaps I express it better by admitting that I can't express it." And see how Anselm plays with negation at III 172 E169 ("I pray that, whenever I receive a letter from your dignity, either I see

course, *this* impossibility result flies in the face of Anselm's purpose; now it looks as if, far from *understanding* God's being and nature, he can't even *think of* it. So later, when Gaunilo finds fault with this procedure, he will have to retract and claim that there is a (weak) sense in which God is thinkable after all. But, for a moment, give the man exactly what he (apparently) wants: the proven existence of something greater than anything thinkable. What then?

It is by thinking that humans give the freest expression to their revolutionary potential. We heard it all from the Frankfurt school people already: Reason is negative, it rejects and violates reality, it *thinks of* better alternatives to it, alternatives that *ought to* come to pass. If a political system is given, or an economic structure, or an educational one, and if its existence is brought up as an argument in its favor, negative reason will rebel against that existence, will find it unjust and ungrounded, will issue a call to dismantle it. After this declaration of war, negative reason's main tool will be the articulation of some new vision, of a land where men and women are free and equal and fully realized, children's growth is not stunted, nobody is bought and sold. And it will be useless to point out that there is no such land, and that there might never be; its conceivability is enough of an indictment, enough of a start in the process of undermining what (sadly) does exist.

It is this process that is blocked by Anselm's impossibility result. A brute presence is affirmed thereby, an existence that is absolutely opaque, and hence absolutely unquestionable. Some have thought of the self's existence as primordial, too, as imposing itself upon consciousness before any conceptualization can be provided of it.[9] But this case is even stronger: no (adequate) conceptualization will *ever* be provided, only pathetic approximations are available, yet this thing cannot be denied, it *is* necessarily. So how can you rebel against it, how can you initiate the critical process of coming up with alternative visions, how can you undermine its facticity, weaken its grip, if you don't even have an idea what the thing is like? No need

---

to whom you are writing, or I not see to whom you are not writing") and III 194 E199 ("the charity, which never does not want what it can and always wants what it can").

[9] This (Cartesian) line is briefly discussed in chapter 1 of Bencivenga (1990), which then proceeds to articulate a different notion of the self—and one that has many points of contact with the notion of God that will ultimately emerge here.

of raising curtains to protect it from sacrilegious looks, of policing the area to make sure that reasoners behave, that they stay within the narrow confines drawn for their activity; there can be no irreverent gazing at what does not reflect our kind of light, no bold challenging of what is never encountered. The activity itself has established its own confines, and thus, in fact, proclaimed its own irrelevance—for what does this domesticated criticism come down to, this meek protest, this cowardly bitching? Is it a joke, or what?[10]

MOTHERS OF INVENTION

By now, the repeated changes of direction in our itinerary have been rationalized. It is *both* rabbits *and* ducks that we are looking at, depending on the angle we decide to take, the story we decide to tell, so it should come as no shock that even this ultimate bastion of decency we just denounced, this supreme knot we found ourselves tying around our necks, can suddenly intimate unsettling alliances, befriend shady characters, maybe prove itself yet another precious implement of inimical reason.

To make sense of the new twist, it may be useful to go back to the beginning, to the early characterization of rational inquiry as play. We decided later that less innocent accounts of this practice may be in order, but we also pointed out that, in the framework in which these other accounts are offered, they need not exclude that earlier one. Indeed, I may add now, one need not even exclude that the only (conscious) attitude the practitioner brings to his inquiry be a gamesome one, since it is not (conscious) attitudes—intentions, if you will—that in this framework give a bunch of moves their logical dignity: it is rather the sense the moves make, primarily from an observer's point of view.[11] So suppose that ours now is an uncon-

[10] One could, of course, think that in this picture anything lesser than God is still accessible to critical reason, which is thus left with plenty of room for its activity. But remember Anselm's suggestions that inquiring into anything lesser than God may be a dangerous and sinful distraction, an expression of evil propria voluntas, and hence such that *external* constraints must be exercised on it (see note 1 of Chapter 1). The conclusion is, then, that those external constraints will be relaxed only when internal ones are effective—when reason demonstrates its own irrelevance.

[11] This reading of agency is articulated in Bencivenga (1991); see also note 3 of Appendix 2.

99

scious spy, a mole that digs holes all through the foundations of a stately building without any awareness of the damage thus inflicted—just for fun. The more holes this truly secret agent digs, the more damage he will inflict; on the other hand, it is also the case that the more holes, the more fun. So open play and hidden war are synergic: whatever encourages and reinforces that play, reinforces and encourages this war.

And now think of play—true, not metaphorical play; the play of a true child. Think of a one-year old crawling on the floor, taking things in his hands, turning them around, pushing and squeezing and mouthing them, making them fall and roll, all in the presence of a majestic maternal figure.[12] In this *Urszene,* all the multifaceted characters of play appear clearly. The child is experimenting with the environment, and doing violence to elements of it, and learning how to move about in there, and running a few risks. So look at the scene more carefully—there may be something to learn from it. See how the child makes a move in a new direction, tentatively, and then looks back at mother, sees her still there, and moves on. See how he reaches a corner, hesitates, turns it, and comes back and shows his face again, repeating the routine several times—and every time mother is still there, and he finally goes back to her. Next time he might be able to turn the corner for good.[13]

Play is destabilizing, it challenges existing equilibria and generates

[12] It is mother as a social role, not as a biological entity, that I am concerned with here, so I would have no problem with a male playing it. See also note 15 below.

[13] Southern (1963) makes a number of important references to the childlike (occasionally childish) nature of Anselm's personality. "The first impression Anselm's writings make is one of youthful brilliance and intensity," he says (33), and remember: "[W]e have nothing which Anselm wrote till he was nearly forty" (ibid.). "With all his theological subtlety and insight into human behaviour he accepted the common views of the time in attributing to the saints of Heaven the manners and morals of preparatory schoolboys" (141). "Probably both Rufus and the bishop [William of St. Calais] . . . were partly nonplussed and partly contemptuous when they discovered that Anselm was as innocent as a child at this game" (149). "[Anselm] took words very seriously and sometimes played with them with the solemnity of a child with its bricks" (352). See also (ibid., 199), where Anselm, after eating pickled eel, bitterly laments that he has eaten raw flesh contrary to the Law, Eadmer reassures him that "[t]he salt has removed the rawness of the flesh," and Anselm replies: "You have saved me from being tortured by the memory of sin." A clear case of parenting, and one that, according to Southern, "[i]n a picturesque way . . . may well give us our best insight into the relations between the archbishop and his biographer."

anxiety. For play to occur, for it to be possible that this (maybe modest) tightrope walking come to pass, there must be ways of dealing with the anxiety, of silencing it.[14] In the primal scene, the resolution of anxiety happens by placing play in a context, against a background that is not itself challenged, that is in fact quite literally *backward*, if forward is the direction of play. The child proceeds to synthesize his world, to try out the different forms that could be imposed on it, and the different sorts of behavior that would follow from each such form, and mother/matter looks on, itself not a play object, not something that requires categorization; a pure presence that antedates all shaping, and makes shaping possible.

We are exiled in this world, Anselm says at IV 99, addressing Pope Urban. We long for the "repose of the celestial fatherland" but are not going to get it. One of the ways we look for this peace and quiet, we know already, is by addressing the murmur of contradiction that keeps rising inside our hearts, and we also know that addressing it is likely to defeat the purpose and generate more and more contradictions, deeper and scarier puzzles. But none of this is going to make any difference in the end; the present game, too, is set against an unquestioned and unquestionable background. God's true nature does not enter the proceedings. We are confronting issues at our scale, attempting to reconcile our miserable understanding with our indestructible faith somehow, so we know that the outcome will be miserable, an expression of our need more than anything else. Somewhat perversely, however, the existence of this barrier becomes a strong incentive for continuing the game, *and for persisting in whatever hidden war is synergic to the game,* in at least two ways: one clearly present in the primal scene described earlier, the other not—though possibly present in richer accounts of the same scene.[15]

---

[14] Anselm gives an eloquent expression of the horror caused by boundlessness at III 59–60 O191–92: "My sins are truly an abyss, since they are incomprehensible by weight and depth, and inestimable by number and immensity. Which abyss is . . . bottomless, since [anyone] who willingly sins deservedly falls *in infinitum.* . . . The abyss of [God's] judgments above me, the abyss of hell below me, the abyss of sins in which I am, and which is in me."

[15] It would be possible to argue, along Freudian lines (and in analogy with the second point to be made below), that the (Oedipal) relation with the mother instigates an unending intellectual curiosity in the child, though one that is displaced onto substitute objects—and indeed, is unending *because* it is displaced. One would then be able to see a stronger resemblance between the child's case and Anselm's. It would turn out that the child, too, is always only searching for the mother (see

First, whatever our moves are, the grantor of supreme peace is going to remain unaffected by them: we are not really playing with God/matter/mother[16] but only, at best, with His reflection in a mirror.[17] So, however bold our insinuations may be, they are merely articulating the limits of our understanding, not the reality of things. To put it bluntly, nobody is going to get hurt.

Second, just because of the incomprehensibility of the (imaginary) focus of our search, the search is to have no end: "[T]he rationale of truth is so large and deep that it cannot be exhausted by mortals" (II 40 H41). God is paradoxical to an extreme: whenever we think we have Him down, He turns around and, in a truly Escherian manner, opens up a new surprising perspective, gives a new humbling demonstration of our intellectual defectiveness.[18]

---

note 10 above), that the "other" things he appears to be searching for are only "reflections in a mirror" of this primal search object (see note 17 below), and that the mother's "background" role does not disconnect her from the child's play—play's "forward" motion establishes metaphorical distance, not growing irrelevance. But I can't pursue this line here any further; for my present purposes, I am happy if my simile is taken in a more superficial way.

[16] At III 40 O153–54, while addressing Jesus in his prayer to Paul, Anselm says: "Truly, Lord, You too mother." Then he goes on, addressing both Jesus and Paul: "Both therefore mothers. For though fathers, also however mothers." The metaphor extends to other authority figures, including Anselm himself. See *Vita* 23: "Thus [Anselm] was a father to the healthy and a mother to the sick, or rather both a father and a mother to the healthy and the sick alike." And see IV 223–24, where abbot Geronton is invited to show "maternal pity." Finally, note Anselm's use of the hen/chicks simile at III 40–41 O153–56 (Christ is the hen) and IV 208 (Queen Matilda is urged to be the hen); at IV 98 the variant nest/chicks occurs (Bec is the nest). Some of these passages are discussed in Bynum (1982), whose emphasis is, however, quite different from mine.

[17] At I 76 M74, Anselm says: "What then? Is it that in some way something is discovered about an incomprehensible thing, and in some way nothing is seen about it? . . . [O]ften we see something not properly, the way the thing itself is, but by means of some likeness or image; as when we contemplate somebody's face in a mirror."

[18] For a good example of this process, see II 180ff S186ff. Anselm sets about inquiring "how indivisible unity and incompatible plurality relate to one another in God." God is one and three, that is, and some consequences of His being one contradict some consequences of His being three; still, we can't give up either tenet of faith. Anselm's strategy is one of minimal revision; that is, (a) he continues to reason about God in ordinary ways, (b) when he gets to a contradiction he rules out one of its horns, but (c) *he keeps the premises of the now abandoned conclusion,* "so that neither unity ever lose its consequence, except where there is some opposition

Which means that our need will never be satisfied, our thirst never quenched, and play will go on forever.[19] "For this very one is among the greatest and most pleasing benefits You bestowed on me, that by making me taste Your sweetness You have excited in me this greed" (III 46 O164). So "[n]ow, my soul, arouse and lift all of your understanding, and consider, as much as you can, of what nature and how great that good is" (I 117 P109).

Faith itself, of course, insofar as it is indestructible, should already bear up the same conclusion; it should already sustain the belief that God is, and that He is more than we could ever (intellectually) handle. But there may be nothing indestructible under the moon after all; in any case it won't hurt to add an extra safety valve, and the ontological argument can be seen as an attempt at procuring such a valve—a rational ground for reason's inevitable failure. Which, in a startling manner, turns out to be just as much of a sinister, sugary invitation to the enemy's ball.

There are other lessons to be learned from this line of thought. One was suggested above, but deserves a clearer statement. At the end of Chapter 1, the interminability of Anselm's search was just a bothersome matter of fact. It created unwelcome problems when trying to decide what he was up to. It raised disturbing suspicions. One may have wished it weren't there. One may have thought there was no intrinsic reason it should be there, no reason we should be using the awkward "interminable search" instead of some other descriptive phrase. Now this matter of fact has been motivated, made to look more like a necessity. We now *understand* (better) what we once (merely) *believed*. We have seen the point of transcendence—of essential apartness, of distinctness in kind—*and* the point of using

---

on the part of relation, nor relation lose what is its own, except where inseparable unity stands in the way." Thus at II 183 S189 the Holy Spirit "necessarily" exists from the Father (just like the Son) "because no opposition is in the way." On the other hand, at II 185 S191, though both the Son and the Holy Spirit exist from the Father, and though one is born and the other proceeds from Him, we cannot say that both are born and both proceed from Him: "[H]ere unity does not have that strength of consequence, because plurality is in the way." Thus ordinary modes of thought and inference must be constantly checked and inhibited in the presence of this strange object, constantly made to reveal their inadequacy, *and constantly stretched.*

[19] Note Anselm's perpetual dissatisfaction with his results and his frequent complaints that he's not had enough time (especially apparent at II 42 H43).

it to set both a target for Anselm's activity (however characterized) and an impassable limit to it. So we can see why transcendence, despite the resulting complications, would have to be there, together with what other characters follow from it: the fictive nature of the transcendent target, and the consequent transformation of rational inquiry into an endless, Sisyphean "journey" (?).

Our second lesson concerns another "matter of fact" that is now ready to be "understood." Why is it that, of our three readings of Anselm's moves, the one of a harmless, self-serving game is the closest to the surface? We had no answer for this question once; now we do. To begin with, consider the distinction between something being a game and something being *just* a game. War is a game, some have said, and so are politics and the stock market and who knows what else, but none of these activities can be considered *just* a game. Calling something *just* a game indicates that, in addition to whatever features make for a game in general (rule-directedness? risk? competition? pleasure?), there is an element of gratuitousness to it. This practice is not to achieve any concrete goal (not directly, at least), not to have any real impact. The features that make for a game in general are the only features that can be called upon to account for something that is *just* a game.

Now consider "the game" of rationalizing our faith. There are two competing authors of the rules of this game, two stern adversaries in the struggle to decide what game it's going to be. One is an adamant defender of the littlest details of the canon, who is playing to build a strong, responsive, and flexible armor around his beliefs, to come up with the final solution to all present and future problems. The other is an agitator, a meddler forever fishing for trouble, a sly conspirator who knows how much damage a few pointed questions can do, even if they get answered, possibly just because they get answered, and in getting answered invade our awareness with their importunate presence. If there is one thing these two opponents must agree on, it is that "the game" should not be treated too seriously or be allowed to infect too much of our ordinary life—not officially, that is. The conservative player knows that it's a risky game, and isolation and detachment are his main tactics for dealing with such risks; so this Q&A activity will have to be played in a make-believe context, tongue in cheek, "academically." If results are obtained, and the system is ever challenged along those lines, the results will be solemnly announced—or, better, it will be solemnly announced that there are results available for inspection, for those (and there are few of them) who are skilled enough to appreciate their significance and value. For a moment, the outcasts working in this enclave will become relevant; then, quickly, they will resume their reclusive, somewhat otherworldly, somewhat laughable status. This way, they will be most useful and least dangerous. On the other hand, it is also in the radical player's best interest not to make waves, more immediately so indeed because there is more power on the other side and hence more of a necessity for him to be deceitful, to masquerade his venomous attacks as harmless entertainment, so as not to raise the anxiety level too high and to have a chance of catching the opposition unawares.

But if so much motivation exists on both sides to make the thing appear as *just* a game, this appearance will become inevitable. There are too many interests sustaining this reassuring picture—conflicting interests as it turns out, which makes for even stronger support. And so we will be told a nice story of devout men in the intimacy of their cloisters deriving saintly, pure joy from a glimpse into the supreme rationality of God's order, and of that being one more gift from Him Whom they love and beseech. It will be yet another example of a quiet sea not revealing all the tempestuous currents streaming below, those currents that by balancing each other out in intricate ways produce precisely that quiet appearance. It will be yet another case of the turbulent, agonistic nature of human experience being sacrificed to superficial clarity; yet another description of "the way things are" that refuses to look into the bloody, messy strife that makes them be that way.

The Law of the Jungle

At six o'clock in the morning on February 17, 1600, members of the Company of St. John the Beheaded showed up at the Nona Tower in Rome, where Giordano Bruno was held prisoner. It was their duty to follow condemned heretics to the stake. Bruno was handed over to them, and they began a long recitation of his errors and exhorted him to recant. Bruno's tongue was locked in a gag, on account of his wicked words. Then, "nude, bound to a stake, accompanied by the mocking solemnity and chanted prayers of his tormentors and held to a terrible silence, [he] was brought forth to the Square of Flowers in Rome" (180).[20] Near the pyre he was shown the image of the Savior, but rejected it angrily by averting his face. Immediately thereafter, he was publicly burnt alive.

This tragedy was the culmination of an erratic life and almost eight years of incarceration, and stands out as arguably the greatest affront ever made to a major philosopher by the established powers. Socrates' death was mild and gentle in comparison. So the question might arise: Was it coincidental? Did Bruno just (unfortunately) find himself at the wrong place at the wrong time, facing the wrong enemy? Maybe so, but the story I told so far has room for a better understanding of all this violence and rage—room for making sense of how much of an affront Bruno himself had represented to the established powers.

It had been suggested before, of course, that we live in an infinite world. Indeed, a long tradition of authors, from Lucretius to Nicholas of Cusa, had articulated this suggestion into imposing, wonderful systems. But it was easy to dismiss that tradition as a mixture of the literary and the mystical, a harmless diversion from more serious intellectual pursuits—as *just* a game, that is. Bruno's situation was different. Partly because of the delicate juncture at which he lived, partly because of the very quality of his work, one could not deny that he was for real. Though not especially gifted as either a mathematician or an experimental scientist, he was current on the latest developments and discussions of the Copernican views, and was able to give his wild, speculative dreams immediate relevance to those developments and discussions. With him more than with any earlier author, the doctrine of the infinite universe was on the verge of becoming official[21]—which, as it turns out, *had* to be the scariest prospect of all for the men at the Holy Office.[22]

Konrad Lorenz (1963) says:

[20] This quote is from Singer (1950), the source of all the information contained in this paragraph.

[21] Arthur O. Lovejoy (1936, 116) says: "Though the elements of the new cosmography had, then, found earlier expression in several quarters, it is Giordano Bruno who must be regarded as the principal representative of the doctrine of the decentralized, infinite, and infinitely populous universe; for he not only preached it throughout Western Europe with the fervor of an evangelist, but also first gave a thorough statement of the grounds on which it was to gain acceptance from the general public." After quoting this passage approvingly, Alexandre Koyré (1957, 39) adds the following: "Indeed, never before has the essential infinitude of space

The layman, misguided by sensationalism in press and film, imagines the relationship between the various "wild beasts of the jungle" to be a bloodthirsty struggle, all against all. In a widely shown film, a Bengal tiger was seen fighting with a python, and immediately afterward the python with a crocodile. With a clear conscience I can assert that such things never occur under natural conditions. What advantage would one of these animals gain from exterminating the other? Neither of them interferes with the other's vital interests. (23)

Most natural selection is intraspecific, and even when interspecific selection occurs the mechanism is the same: species X supplants species Y not by attacking it directly but by handling the same ecological niche more effectively—as the dingo did with many marsupials in Australia. Thus a species's most dangerous enemies are not its predators but its competitors; it is the latter, not the former, that can bring it to extinction.

Lorenz (1963, 1973) also proposes to apply an evolutionary model to human cultures. If this model is accepted, the following will sound like a sensible claim: A cultural trait A's most dangerous enemies are (not so much the agents that attack it directly, but rather) other traits that perform the same function(s) as A. If A has a job to do, and if the culture depends on that job being done, it will be pointless to simply try to extirpate A; even if the effort were successful, the chances are that the culture would be doomed as well. On the other hand, when something else is found that does the same job just as well, or maybe even better, A's fate is not so sure. There

---

been asserted in such an outright, definite and conscious manner." Of Nicholas of Cusa, Koyré says: "[W]e must recognise . . . that, without going far beyond him, it is impossible to link [his cosmological conceptions] with astronomical science or to base upon them a 'reformation of astronomy.' This is probably why his conceptions were so utterly disregarded by his contemporaries, and even by his successors for more than a hundred years. No one, not even Lefèvre d'Etaples who edited his works, seems to have paid much attention to them" (18). And of another competitor for priority rights, Thomas Digges, Koyré says: "Digges puts his stars into a theological heaven; not into an astronomical sky. . . . [H]e maintains the separation between our world—the world of the sun and the planets—and the heavenly sphere, the dwelling-place of God, the celestial angels, and the saints" (38–39).

22 Singer (1950, 179) relates the following account of Bruno's bearing under judgment (from a letter written by a Gaspar Schopp of Breslau): "When the verdict had been declared, . . . Bruno with a threatening gesture addressed his judges: 'Perchance you who pronounce my sentence are in greater fear than I who receive it.'"

is of course inertia in the cultural as in the biological realm; cultural traits may survive their usefulness as much as biological ones. But not forever, not necessarily, and not under pressure.

In the culture of which Anselm was such a distinguished representative, the ineffable, unimaginable, and inconceivable God had a job to do; indeed, as we have found, more than one. He was at the same time the supreme barrier beyond which irreverent inquiry could not peek[23] and the supreme incentive to continue with that inquiry without (too much) fear. His one person satisfied two dialectically counterposed human needs: the one for novelty, surprise, and change, and the one for stability and order. But now an infinite ungodly object, greater than humans can conceive, looms over the horizon, and suddenly it's anybody's game. The arguments for the infinity of this object are still theological in nature, and the object's appearance is still mixed up with divinity in a big pantheistic soup, but those are inessential features, remnants of (by now) antiquated modes of expression. The thing can stand on its own, and if it can, eventually it will. At that point, God will become an embarrassing epicycle, and deleting Him from the picture will have all the underwhelming quality of an administrative decision.[24] For there will be, at that point, a competing arena for play, an arena without boundaries for play without end; indeed, an arena whose "true" noumenal nature may be just as out of reach as that of the Archetypal Parental Figure who traditionally dominated the field, and hence just as much of a perpetually unsolvable puzzle designed to bring out all the mythmaking powers of our being. As for those other, more conservative tendencies that the supreme parent also satisfied, they will have to be taken care of by other means, when the traditional equilibrium is undermined and a new distribution of (cultural) labor becomes necessary. In the meantime, it's not to be wondered at that any moves to undermine that equilibrium in the name of the emerging com-

---

[23] In the first draft of the *Epistola de incarnatione verbi,* Anselm says of Roscelin: "Therefore his understanding passes beyond God" (I 289). And that is the end of a paragraph. In the final draft, he goes back and adds: "which no understanding can do" (II 18 l21).

[24] A significant statement in this regard is made by P. F. Strawson (1966) in the opening paragraph of his chapter on God: "It is with very moderate enthusiasm that a twentieth-century philosopher enters the field of philosophical theology, even to follow Kant's exposure of its illusions" (207).

petitor should be vehemently resisted by the status quo. By fire, if need be.

In recent years, modernity has often been contrasted with *post-modernity*, where the key elements of contrast are the presence versus the absence of grand, explanatory narratives, and the integration versus the fragmentation of the subjects of those narratives. Not as much emphasis has been placed on the fact that modernity itself is inaugurated by a cultural fragmentation of epochal scope. It is this fragmentation that I was beginning to articulate in the previous paragraph. In premodern culture, there is great integration at the unit level—or, maybe better, the unit of integration is smaller. For the believer, God is, as I have been arguing, both an authority figure and a liberating one, so in his relation with this ultimate Thou the believer finds freedom and constraint at once: intellectual excitement together with a harsh negative judgment on the power of the intellect, food for thought together with strict dietary prescriptions. This high level of interpenetration makes for a highly stable system, both in the positive sense that the system will be around for a long time and in the negative one that it will tend not to improve (to be "rationalized") a whole lot. Reason will be *just a game,* an innocent, childish, frivolous pastime that is not expected to generate any fallout.

When intellectual freedom is found independently, on the other hand, in something that is not itself an authority figure, important consequences will follow. One was hinted at above: authority will have to come from somewhere else—nature, tradition, the general will, or whatever. But there is also another consequence: if two different cultural traits do these different cultural jobs, we shouldn't expect to find both traits strongly represented in the same individuals. It is possible, of course, but that would be an empirical matter; it's just as likely to be different people who incarnate play and discipline. Indeed, it's *more* likely to be different people, once it *can* be, because of how much more efficient each of them is at the one thing he does when he need not worry too much about extraneous considerations.

So it will be mostly scientists who play in the infinite field now made available, with not too much piety to impede their action, and it will be mostly politicians and bureaucrats who act as custodians of the social order and if necessary impose some needed restraint on the players' most inconsiderate moves. The integration among these conflicting tendencies will have to be found at a superindividual level, within society as a whole, and it will (tend to) be integration of a more unstable sort. Without the internal balancing factor that religious reverence provided, players-scientists will get going at their game to an extreme and will identify with it totally. With that much drive and dedication, they will eventually cross the threshold where the game does make a difference "out there," indeed a difference that will eventually explode and force the political and administrative powers to constantly rewrite directions for a landscape that keeps changing before their very eyes. Rationalizing the system will become "the thing" now, and it will be a matter of not rationalizing it too fast and too destructively—of not being eaten up by the game, in a way that was impossible when it was *just* a game.

Think all of this away, if you can. The single-minded, ruthless pursuit of new, "original" ideas. The vindication of those ideas by their practical application and success. Their becoming a product like any other; their being owned and bought and sold. The farce of a universal means of exchange dictating the "value" of everything. The nightmare of a power that proves itself by turning hills into flatland, and then again flatland into hills.

Strain your imagination to think of a little man in a little cell, one of many sleepless nights. He has worked hard all day keeping things and people in line, *the* line—the only one, the one that has always been. He has taught others by word and by example how to be faithful to the old ordinances; he has shown them that you do it slowly and patiently, paying careful attention to minutiae, trying to duplicate routines without fault. He has withstood wild ambitions and silly prides, firmly rejected threats and enticements, made sure that, as far as he is concerned, everything will stay immutably itself.

Now, however, it is not time for work, for the "sterile impediments" (III 154 E146) and the "vile and sterile . . . occupations" (III 163 E158) of everyday life. Now his only company, and his only audience, is his God. Now he can rejoice. Because this God is infinite, will never let him down, prove Himself trivial, let Himself be exhausted. "If I say all that I will be able to contrive, still it won't be comparable to what the thing is" (III 78 O223). As human words are stretched in the wake of that Word which is identical with Its Object, they will always fall short, so there will always be room for more stretching, for more taxing of one's resources, for asking more

110

of one's feeble mind. And this God is safe. Nothing we can do will affect—not to mention damage—Him. Even when we want to offend Him, and proceed accordingly, we can't do it. We do evil, of course, we do a disservice and a dishonor to ourselves, but this fly can't expect That Mountain to even feel its sting. He is impassible, inaccessible to injury. So it will be all right to voice one's most intimate worries: His benevolent presence will be untouched, indeed smile at these pious efforts, feel the love behind them.

Thank you, God, for this hour of bliss. Our desire for knowledge, for a word matching the truth of Your Word, almost lost us once, and You came down and relieved us of our burden. And now You even give me so much of an image of You, so much knowledge and understanding of Your ineffable essence. It is faulty knowledge, I know, and defective understanding; I could use my very reason to prove that. My very reason tells me that You are far too much for it. Still, this pale, confused grasping is some reflection of You, and You give it to me though You know I don't deserve it, just so that I can rejoice. And, because of how pale and confused it is, I can continue to strive and pray, and maybe tomorrow You will give me something else, a little bit better. You will keep my mind alive one more day, and my body, too, since it, too, needs this sort of food more than any other: needs tension, and encouragement, and hope.

Fade to black.

111

The Logic of an Illusion

Oₙₑ ₜₕᵢₙ𝔤 nobody will deny, when it comes to the logic of the ontological argument, is that it is difficult to figure it out. The argument's persistent attractiveness is evidence that there is something convincing about it, and yet many think of it as a kind of sleight-of-hand performance and are forever searching for where the trick might be. This situation suggests to me that there may be a complicated network of principles, and possibly some basic tension among these principles, in the deep grammar of the argument, and that the surface simplicity of its formulation in the *Proslogion* may be delusive. So I thought it might prove helpful to look for a *less* simple formulation, where the various moves involved might show more clearly, with the intent of eventually bringing the results of this analysis to bear upon the more traditional, deceptively straightforward version.[1] Here, then, is a report of what I found.

My text is a passage from *Responsio editoris,* which reads as follows:

> But let us assume that [that, than which a greater cannot be thought] not be, provided at least it can be thought. But whatever can be thought and is not, if it were to be, it would not be "that, than which a greater cannot be thought." Therefore, if "that, than which a greater

---

[1] Starting at least with Malcolm (1960), analytic philosophers have often distinguished two versions of the argument in the *Proslogion*: one (in chapter II) attempting to prove the existence of God, and the other (in chapter III) attempting to prove His *necessary* existence. Anselm, they occasionally acknowledge, might not have been sensitive to the distinction; still, the latter version is more promising than the former as a place to look for a *sound* argument. I think that there is something to this claim, though I cannot accept it as it stands. In my view, there is indeed a role for necessary existence here, and for an essential contribution on the part of chapter III. This contribution, however, consists in presenting not an alternative, independent argument, but rather an auxiliary one in support of a key step in the *main* argument, given in chapter II. (*This* is why Anselm would not recognize the distinction his analytic critics talk about.) So a secondary aim of the present appendix is that of clarifying the relations between chapters II and III of the *Proslogion* (see notes 8 and 15 below, and the attending text).

cannot be thought" were to be, it would not be that, than which a greater cannot be thought; which is exceedingly absurd. (I 131 P124)[2]

A number of statements in this argument are counterfactuals, so to simplify matters I am going to utilize a possible-world rewrite of such statements. I am not, however, going to decide here among the various competing possible-world semantics of counterfactuals; mine is only a terminological choice. Using this terminology, I will now provide a reformulation of the argument (where "that, than which a greater cannot be thought" is abbreviated by "X").

(1) One can think of X.
(2) Therefore, there is a (thinkable) world w where X exists.
(3) Now suppose that X does not exist in the real world.
(4) Then, in w, something greater than X can be thought.
(5) But this is a logical falsehood.

The above is a reductio argument, and (3) is the premise to be proven absurd, which makes it unobjectionable. Something might be the matter with the other premise, (1), of course; one might wonder how strongly "think of" is to be read. But the weakest possible reading will do, for my present purposes. I will take it that the argument succeeds if it (at least) establishes that God exists, without making Him any less incomprehensible or inconceivable than He was before the argument. So, through most of this appendix, I will be concentrating on the three inferential steps, (2), (4), and (5). First, consider (5). What is the logical falsehood referred to here? Clearly, it is the following:

(6) That, than which a greater cannot be thought, is such that a greater than it can be thought.

And (6) is a logical falsehood if and only if the following is a logical truth:

(7) That, than which a greater cannot be thought, is such that a greater than it cannot be thought.

[2] I am certainly not the first one to notice this passage: Malcolm (1960, 48–49), for example, quotes from the same paragraph what is in essence a variant of the same argument (partly quoted in note 8 below), and says that it "adds [an] acute point." But, to my knowledge, nobody has considered the passage as crucial as I do, or drawn the same moral from it.

Now (7) sounds familiar, of course, because it is on some such basis that the traditional ontological argument is ordinarily accounted for, but there is an important difference here from what happens in ordinary analyses; that is, in the argument I am considering, (7) is applied to an *existent* object (that, than which a greater cannot be thought, does exist in *w*),[3] and with this qualification it is difficult to find anything wrong with it. In other words, (7) is an instance of the Principle of Self-Predication,

(8) The P is (a) P,[4]

and there are all sorts of problems with (8) in general—problems with round squares that are not round, and the like. However, (8) seems undeniably true *when the P exists,* or, to put it otherwise, the Restricted Principle of Self-Predication,

(9) *If the P exists*, then the P is (a) P,

seems to be a logical truth. If somebody existent is *the tallest man alive,* one does not see how he could help being taller than any other man, and hence, if (9) is the principle invoked to justify (5), the justification is a plausible one. Gaunilo, incidentally, would agree: "For it is necessary that it first be made certain to me that this greater thing truly exists somewhere, and then indeed from the fact that it is greater than everything it will doubtless [follow] that it also subsists in itself" (I 128 P118–19).

Within traditional discussions of the ontological argument, what we tend to see is a mirror image of this issue. For there, of course, the principle invoked is (8) in its most general form, and then a battle is fought over whether existence can be legitimately thought to fall within the scope of the variable "P"; over whether, that is, existence is a predicate or not. Here the problem is avoided by building exis-

---

[3] The key phrase in this regard is the counterfactual hypothesis "if it were to be."

[4] For this to be the case, it is essential that, when Anselm says "if 'that, than which a greater cannot be thought' were to be," we read him as meaning "if 'that, than which a greater cannot be thought' were to exist *and still be* 'that, than which a greater cannot be thought' "—and hence as ruling out the possibility that, if what is *actually* that, than which a greater cannot be thought, were to exist, it might no longer be properly described that way. In other words, we must assume that, within the scope of "what can(not) be thought," Anselm includes what can(not) be thought *in any thinkable world*. But that this is Anselm's intended reading is suggested, at least, by considerations of charity: a different reading would make the argument hopeless.

tence into the principle, but that is not all, I would argue. If we now reverse the order of conceptual priority between (8) and (9), and think (not so much of (9) as a restricted form of (8), but rather) of (8) as an unwarranted extrapolation from (9), we can get a lot clearer about what works and what doesn't within this overall strategy.

The background for the move I am recommending is to be found in Bencivenga (1987). There I point out that Kant's monumental turnabout consisted in a rearranging of logical space; specifically, of the relations of logical dependence holding among various key concepts. Traditional transcendental (which for me simply amounts to "conceptual") realism was based on the notion of an object, so this notion was itself not defined, and every other notion (for example, that of an experience) was defined by reference to it; Kantian transcendental idealism, on the other hand, is based on the notion of an experience, *and the notion of an object is to be characterized by reference to experiences*.

To see the relevance of this background to the issue at hand, consider first of all that, as I argued elsewhere,[5] from the point of view of transcendental realism the notion of an object and that of an *existent* object come to the same thing. The transcendental realist could well say, as in fact Quine (1948) did, that "[a] curious thing about the ontological problem is its simplicity. It can be put in three Anglo-Saxon monosyllables: 'What is there?' It can be answered, moreover, in a word—'Every*thing*'—and everyone will accept this answer as true" (21, italics mine).

Now consider a statement of the form

(10) The *P* is *Q*.

On the surface of it, this statement is a predication; more precisely, it predicates the property *Q* of the object designated by "the *P*." But this can only happen if there is an object designated by "the *P*," that is (for the realist), *if the P exists*. If there exists no such thing as the *P*, then you can't say anything about it, and what appears to be a predication is not; the surface grammar of (10) must be delusive, and you must in fact be saying something else. Therefore, within transcendental realism, (8)—as a logical principle, not as a delusive grammatical appearance—can only mean (9), and since (9) is hardly questionable, (8)'s credentials will be just as strong. (And the whole

[5] In chapter 2 of Bencivenga (1989).

issue of whether existence is a predicate or not reduces to the following: predicating existence of anything is at best trivial because something would not be *a thing* if it didn't exist.)[6]

For the transcendental idealist, on the other hand, a statement of the form (10) is perfectly legitimate whether or not the P exists; for him it is not true, as Russell (1918–19, 243) put it, that "a name has got to name something or it is not a name."[7] A name must have a certain role in language, and in the end some of the expressions that have this role will be found to name existent objects and some will not. So, for the transcendental idealist, (8) does not mean (9), but this also entails that for him (8) is not an attractive principle at all; a brief reflection on round squares that are not round and the like will convince him that there are no good reasons to believe in its truth—though of course he may still believe in the truth of (9), which for him is clearly *not* the same thing as (8). In conclusion, the argument in the *Responsio* seems to bring out the Principle of Self-Predication in a form in which it is in fact an acceptable principle, and the only plausible reason why one might think of the other—more commonplace—form is as a convenient abbreviation (within transcendental realism) for this more basic one.

Turn now to step (2). One way we can begin to work toward its justification is by referring to something like the following Principle of Intentionality:

(11) If Y thinks of Z, then Z is an object Y thinks of.

If you accept (11), it will not take a whole lot of arguing to expand it into something like

(12) If Y thinks of Z, then Z is an object existing in a world
     Y thinks of.

(At the very least, the relevant world can be one containing *only* Z, though for reasons that will become apparent shortly it is better to conceive of it as richer than that—and as more similar to the real world.) And (12) would be enough to justify (2). So the question is, How acceptable is (11)?

Return to the two sides involved in Kant's Copernican revolution.

---

[6] On this issue, see Bencivenga (1980).

[7] This Russellian statement is quoted and discussed in chapter 9 of Bencivenga (1989).

For the transcendental realist, (11) is way too strong: I can think of all sorts of absurdities, but this doesn't make them objects. At best, I can say that I *try* to think of objects then, but do not succeed (whatever *that* means). For the transcendental idealist, on the other hand, (11) is a perfectly respectable principle; for him, objects enter the conceptual picture as objects *of (some) experiences,* for example, objects of discourse, or of desire, or—as in this case—of thought. But, of course, for him (11) says nothing really exciting. To talk of an object here (of an *intentional* object, to use the most common terminology) is simply to bring out the directional character of this experience, and hence it is simply to rephrase what was already said in (1)—as we would have to expect if this is a logical step. In logic, I was told once, every step is bound to be either trivially right or interestingly wrong, and this dichotomy has a clear application to the present case: (11) is an ambitious but totally unwarranted claim for the realist, and an unquestionable but totally flat one for the idealist. To summarize the analysis so far, then, the realist has to part ways with this argument here, though the idealist may want to go further, since he's got no problem with (11) and is still buying (9).

So let us now turn to the last inferential step in the argument, (4). What could be the justification for this? Something like the following subargument is probably what Anselm intended:[8]

(13) = (3)
(14) In w, one can think of something that exists in all worlds.
(15) Y is greater than Z if Y exists in all worlds and Z does not.
(16) = (4).

How does this argument fare? (14) requires extending to w thinking abilities that we are familiar with in the real world, but this is not a large concession.[9] As for (15), it may be taken as definitional of

[8] To see this, it is useful to consider the two sentences preceding the passage quoted on pp. 113–14: "But whatever can be thought and is not: if it were to be, it could fail to be either in fact or in the understanding. Therefore, if at least it can be thought, it cannot not be 'that, than which a greater cannot be thought' " (I 131 P124).

[9] After all, semantics for counterfactuals in general agree in making the relevant worlds as similar as possible to the real one.

"greater than,"[10] so the question reduces to whether (16) follows from premises (13)–(15). And here the controversy between the realist and the idealist becomes relevant once again.

For the realist, objects are conceptually independent of experiences: they come (logically) first, *and then* possibly (and inessentially) one has experiences of them. The present situation, admittedly, is rather peculiar: we are inquiring into what the case would be if X *were* an object. Still, the only way the realist can deal with this situation is by importing into it his ordinary conceptual strategies: if X were an object, it *would be* as independent of any experience as objects are in general supposed to be. Moving from counterfactual to possible-world jargon, suppose that X is an object in w and ask yourself: Does X have (in w) the property of being such that a greater than it cannot be thought? Well, can one think (in w) of something W that exists in all worlds? Yes. But that entails (definitionally) being able to think (in w) of something W greater than anything that only exists in some worlds,[11] hence in particular (given our assumptions about X) greater than X.[12] End of story: X does not have the required property. We know that the realist would have serious problems admitting that X *is* an object—in w or anywhere. But if we separate the two issues (that is, separate the analyses of inferential steps (2) and (4)), then we can see that the realist would have no problem with *the present issue*.[13]

---

[10] Which is not to say that (15) is (necessarily) the *whole* definition of "greater than," but only that this definition will (at least) *include* (15).

[11] This being a definitional entailment simplifies matters considerably, since it lets us make the relevant substitution without having to worry about the status of W, in analogy with the following: Being able to think of a round square entails being able to think of a four-sided figure, whatever the status of round squares might be. Which is just as well, given how troublesome the status of W is for a realist—even in w, W is still only an object of thought.

[12] Note that the realist need not argue that anybody in w *thinks* of X as not existing in the real world, or as such that something greater than it can be thought. All that is needed is that *in fact* something greater than X can be thought (in w). To put it otherwise, X has a given status (in w), and being able to think of something greater than X means being able to think of something *with a higher status* (whatever one in fact thinks of X), in analogy with the following: If (a) Y is mortal, (b) I can think of something immortal, and (c) being immortal is (definitionally) greater than being mortal, then (d) I can think of something greater than Y— *whether or not I think that Y is mortal*.

[13] An alternative way of formulating this point is as follows: If the realist takes a to be an object, it is natural for him to consider any occurrence of "a" referential,

Take the idealist, then, who does admit that X is an object. Can he make the same moves? Not at all. To be an object, for him, is to be the object-of-an-experience, and the normal case is when such an (intentional) object cannot be "detached" from the experience and considered—and manipulated—independently of it. At times, of course, such detaching is possible; for example, if I became convinced that the present experience of seeing a computer is internally consistent and well connected with the rest of (my) experiences, I might detach its object (the computer) and talk about it *simpliciter.* In general, this operation requires a lot of work, and if the work is not done the object will remain buried within its experience.[14] But it is precisely this kind of work that the ontological argument is supposed to do. If the argument is successful, we will have proved that God exists and will be able to detach Him from our experience of, for example, thinking of Him. Therefore, it is a petitio principii to expect the work to be done before the argument is concluded (that is, to expect one of the crucial steps in the argument to depend on successful completion of the work).

More specifically, X is the object-of-a-thought. I have not yet established that this thought makes any sense—a necessary, though not sufficient, condition for being able to consider its object independently of it. And if no such independence is forthcoming, how can I reason about this object and decide, for example, that something greater than it can (or cannot) be thought? Thinking of X as not existing in the real world, thinking of it as existing in w, and thinking of thinking (in w) of something that exists in all worlds are all different experiences, and I don't even know that they are consistent with one another, much less that they have the kind of connectedness required for detachment. I can, of course, *think* that this is the case, and that the relevant comparison between X and something else W becomes possible (or, indeed, that the comparison is made), but those would be yet *other* experiences, whose consistency *with the former* (or even with themselves) totally escapes me (and *must*

---

that is, to think of any context in which "a" occurs as a transparent one—which is precisely why he has so many problems with (substitutivity in) *opaque* contexts. And, of course, if the present contexts of occurrences of "X" are taken to be transparent, the inferences in the text are perfectly legitimate.

[14] A good example of what I mean by an object being buried within the experience of which it is an object is given by objects of desire. See chapter 7 of Bencivenga (1989).

escape me, under the circumstances; I don't see how this matter could even be addressed, not to mention resolved, with anything like the tools mobilized by Anselm's argument, in any of its versions). For the idealist, then, the whole project suggested by subargument (13)–(16) is a nonstarter.

The conclusion of this analysis is as follows: Of the inferential steps (2), (4), and (5), one is acceptable to both realists and idealists, but the other two are only acceptable to one party, *and not the same party in the two cases,* so that in the end neither party can find the argument convincing.

I promised that I would apply the results of my analysis to the more traditional and simpler version of the ontological argument. So here is the relevant passage from the *Proslogion*:

> For if it is even in the understanding alone, it can be thought to be also in the thing, which is greater. Therefore, if that, than which a greater cannot be thought, is in the understanding alone, that very thing, than which a greater cannot be thought, is [one] than which a greater can be thought. But certainly this cannot be. (I 101–2 P94)

It is not immediately clear here that the principle of self-predication we need is the reasonable (9), not the unacceptable (8). However, looking at this argument from the point of view of the other one, we can see it as mobilizing two worlds: the real one, of which we have to prove X to be a citizen (by proving it to exist "in the thing"), and a world w of which X is already a citizen (by existing "in the understanding"). Then we can see Anselm as comparing the two worlds and trying to establish (with an assist from chapter III)[15] a contradiction *in the latter;* that is, trying to establish that in w, where

---

[15] The reason the assist is necessary is that it is not at all clear here *why* (a) "to also exist in the thing" is greater than (b) "to exist in the understanding alone"— and it is precisely such lack of clarity that makes this version "deceptively straight-forward" (see p. 113 above). Is Anselm claiming that (a) is greater than (b) because existing is greater than not existing, or rather because necessarily existing is greater than contingently existing? (A similar ambiguity is noted, but not resolved, by Malcolm, 1960, 42.) One small piece of evidence in favor of the second reading is provided by the qualification "also"—Lat.: *et*—in "also in the thing," which might seem unnecessary in the first reading, but it is hardly conclusive evidence. The argument in the *Responsio* resolves the ambiguity and clarifies the relation between chapters II and III of the *Proslogion*; how the latter, that is, is supposed to fill in what the former left open.

X does exist, X is not that, than which a greater cannot be thought, because supposedly it does not exist "in the thing."

You might see some sense in this discussion, and still find it somewhat gratuitous. First, it might indeed be possible to see the argument in the *Proslogion* from the point of view of the one in the *Responsio,* but why should we? What do we gain by seeing it that way? Second, my analysis of the argument in the *Responsio* could be duplicated without bringing out the whole business of transcendental realism and idealism. Restricted self-predication and intentionality are certainly nothing new, and as for the third inferential step I considered one could make much the same points made above by talking (for example) about *de re* and *de dicto* contexts, and seeing Anselm as involved in some kind of confusion between the two. So, once again, what do we gain by putting it in the grand terms of the Copernican revolution?

I started out by saying that there are two aspects to the ontological argument. One is that many think it's a trick, and must not be sound. The other is that virtually everybody finds something attractive about it, and hence in spite of centuries of criticism we are still debating it. Any satisfactory analysis of the argument would have to account for *both* of these aspects. And here my feeling is that appeal to a simple confusion, or to any sort of purely logical mistake, is not going to be enough.

In the first *Critique* (298–300), Kant points out that a logical illusion—one caused by a logical mistake—is dispelled as soon as the mistake is made explicit. Suppose I tell you the following:

(17) No grammarian can be conceived without a reference to grammar.
(18) Humans can be conceived without a reference to grammar.
(19) Therefore, no grammarian is human.

You may be puzzled for a while and experience the logical equivalent of motion sickness, but when I patiently point out to you (along the lines of I 148 G42–43) that (a) the expression "can be conceived" is ambiguous here, since it may be taken to mean "can be conceived *as a grammarian*" or "can be conceived *as a human,*" and (b) though humans certainly can be conceived *as humans* with no reference to grammar, they cannot be conceived *as grammarians* with no reference to grammar, you will get the distinction and will no longer be fooled.

Indeed, you will probably become able to recognize similar traps in other contexts as well.

There is of course the possibility that the purely logical mistake made by Anselm—the mistake whose discovery would make things once and forever transparent—has not been discovered yet, so those who think that they can do better than the tradition are welcome to keep on trying. I prefer to take another tack, and think of what is involved in the ontological argument as a *transcendental* illusion in Kant's sense; that is, one that depends (not just on a mistake, but) on the use of principles that are necessary for us to function properly, and hence one that will not be avoided even after it's been detected. We will continue to have it and will have to continually (and critically) remind ourselves of its delusional character.

This is the point of bringing out transcendental realism and idealism. For many of us (indeed all, if Kant is right), these are poles of a perpetual, necessary oscillation. We live in a world of things, not of experiences, and hence at the empirical level, when we are not involved in rational reflection, realism ("things first") is the natural standpoint, so if we don't check ourselves it will be natural for us to apply it, automatically and unreflectively, even where it is *not* productive to do so. The latter is the case within rational reflection. When it comes to justifying our experience, to inquiring about its legitimacy, starting with things—natural, irresistible as it may be— is not going to go very far, and idealism ("experiences first") can get us one or two steps further. Both points of view are required, and so is the constant switching between them *and* the illusions the switching generates. If I am right, it is exactly this switching that is involved in the ontological argument. The figure the argument draws is neither a rabbit nor a duck, since it makes no sense in either paradigm, but the moves made in drawing it are familiar ones, they are legitimate in one paradigm *or* the other. Each move per se is fine; they just don't all belong together, and if you put them together you get a big mess. But that big mess matches the big mess we are, the conflictual nature of our various concerns. So there is no way of avoiding it, though every time we are fooled we may, by using some such strategy as I suggested here, critically remind ourselves of what the problem is.

Esoteric Doctrines

A NUMBER of authors have proposed "esoteric doctrine" interpretations of classical texts.[1] The essence of these interpretations is as follows (where "*A*" stands for any author and "*W*" for any of his works):

(1) *A* did not truly mean everything he said in *W*; indeed, his true meaning is sometimes quite the opposite of his literal one.

(2) However, his true meaning can be found hidden under the literal one; there are enough signs of it in *W* that one can reconstruct it accurately.

(3) Such signs are not to be understood by the general readership, but only by a limited group of initiated people.

(4) In conclusion, *W* expresses (at least) *two* doctrines: an exoteric one for the general readership, and an esoteric one for the initiated.

From the point of view that I have been developing in this book, "esoteric doctrine" interpretations represent an interesting compromise between (what I perceive as) the essential multiplicity of any text on the one hand and a persistently realist attitude on the other. For the idealist, the spatiotemporal manifold is intrinsically ambiguous. In general, many patterns will be identifiable in it *and in any portion of it,* and it's perfectly possible that more than one of them will display those characters of coherence and connectedness that make a pattern objective, that is, the manifestation *of an object* (keeping in mind that all such judgments are revisable and context-dependent). Now consider a text. Being a meaningful occurrence, the text is supposed to manifest more than just its own objectivity; there is also supposed to be a meaning agency that manifests itself through the text. That is, there is supposed to be an agency X such that (a) X has caused the being of the text, and (b) some of the structure of X can be gleaned from the structure of the text. Ordinarily,

[1] For a good example, see Caton (1973).

this agency is taken to be the author,[2] but the author (as, indeed, the text) is a portion of the manifold, so it's possible that there is more than one (objective) account of him (or of his text). Different people, differently disposed, might well be more receptive to different accounts—ready to pick up *this* regularity in the author (and text) rather than *that* one.[3] And it might at times prove useful to bring out several accounts (as I tried to do here for Anselm) and show their mutual interplay.

Now think of a realist trying to describe this situation. His world is made of a unique collection of (uniquely determined) objects; subjects are among these objects, and authors are among these subjects. Also, causation is unique: there is only *one* cause[4] (however complex) for any event (or for the being of any object). Therefore, if texts manifest their authors, they manifest them uniquely; the one thing a text means is the (one) thing its author *meant by* it. If two conflicting "meanings" are to be discovered in a text—and sometimes that's exactly what one would want to say, since both "make sense" of the text—both must have been meant by the author and, since the author could only *truly* have meant *one* of two conflicting messages, one of them he must have meant truly *and the other falsely.* I noticed on page 81 above that, in the model I work with, "deception falls off as a useless concept." What we see here is a mirror image of that conclusion: For the opposite model, deception is often a necessity. Often, multiplicity can be read in a text only by importing the notion of (intentionally) *lying* into it.

[2] Not always, however; sometimes one believes that it is (say) the author's culture, or the economic structure of his society, that finds expression in the text. And then the realist faces a problem analogous to the one mentioned below; the problem, that is, of how to reconcile the author's "intentions" with the workings of the other meaning agency thus brought forth. Usually, the solution is also analogous: deception is invoked, this time in the form of *self*-deception (on the author's part).

[3] This theme is analyzed in chapter 5 of Bencivenga (1989), which can now be seen as a step in the gradual shifting process from one paradigm to the other. Concentrating on the responses by the readers and on their multiplicity, as I do there, is instrumental in finally admitting the multiplicity of the object itself that is to be read.

[4] One should add here: *if any* (though the addition is of no relevance in the present context). For it seems also possible to the realist, of course, that in some cases there may be no cause at all, that some events (or the being of some things) should be ascribed to pure chance.

✣ Bibliography ✣

Whenever a translation, a new edition, or a new printing is cited below, it is to it that references are made in the book.

Barth, Karl
  (1958) *Fides Quaerens Intellectum*. 2d edition. Translated by I. Robertson. Cleveland & New York: Meridian Books, 1960.
Bencivenga, Ermanno
  (1979) "On Good and Bad Arguments." *Journal of Philosophical Logic* 8:247–59.
  (1980) "Again on Existence as a Predicate." *Philosophical Studies* 37: 125–38.
  (1987) *Kant's Copernican Revolution*. New York: Oxford University Press.
  (1989) *Looser Ends*. Minneapolis: University of Minnesota Press.
  (1990) *The Discipline of Subjectivity: An Essay on Montaigne*. Princeton: Princeton University Press.
  (1991) *La libertà: un dialogo*. Milan: Il Saggiatore.
Bynum, Caroline Walker
  (1982) *Jesus as Mother: Studies in the Spirituality of the High Middle Ages*. Berkeley & Los Angeles: University of California Press.
Carnap, Rudolf
  (1934) *Logische Syntax der Sprache*. Translated by A. Smeaton. London: Routledge & Kegan Paul, 1937.
Caton, Hiram
  (1973) *The Origin of Subjectivity: An Essay on Descartes*. New Haven: Yale University Press.
Frege, Gottlob
  (1892a) "Über Sinn und Bedeutung." Translated by M. Black in Frege (1984), 157–77.
  (1892b) "Über Begriff und Gegenstand." Translated by P. Geach in Frege (1984), 182–94.
  (1897a) "Über die Begriffsschrift des Herrn Peano und meine eigene." Translated by V. Dudman in Frege (1984), 234–48.
  (1897b) "Logik." Translated by P. Long and R. White in Frege (1979), 126–51.
  (1906a) "Über Schoenflies: *Die logischen Paradoxien der Mengenlehre*." Translated by P. Long and R. White in Frege (1979), 176–83.
  (1906b) "Einleitung in die Logik." Translated by P. Long and R. White in Frege (1979), 185–96.

(1915) "Meine grundlegenden logischen Einsichten." Translated by P. Long and R. White in Frege (1979), 251–52.

(1918) "Der Gedanke." Translated by P. Geach and R. Stoothoff in Frege (1984), 351–72.

(1924) "Zahl." Translated by P. Long and R. White in Frege (1979), 265–66.

(1969) *Nachgelassene Schriften.* Edited by H. Hermes et al. Hamburg: Felix Meiner.

(1979) *Posthumous Writings.* Edited by H. Hermes et al. Oxford: Basil Blackwell.

(1984) *Collected Papers on Mathematics, Logic, and Philosophy.* Edited by B. McGuinness. Oxford: Basil Blackwell.

Henry, Desmond Paul

(1967) *The Logic of Saint Anselm.* Oxford: Clarendon Press.

Hodges, Andrew

(1983) *Alan Turing: The Enigma.* London: Burnett Books.

Hopkins, Jasper

(1972) *A Companion to the Study of St. Anselm.* Minneapolis: University of Minnesota Press.

Horkheimer, Max, and Theodor W. Adorno

(1944) *Dialektik der Aufklärung.* Translated by J. Cumming. New York: Herder and Herder, 1972. Reprinted by Continuum (New York, 1991).

Kant, Immanuel

(1787) *Kritik der reinen Vernunft.* 2d edition. Translated by N. Kemp Smith. London: Macmillan, 1929. Reprinted by St. Martin's Press (New York, 1965).

Koyré, Alexandre

(1957) *From the Closed World to the Infinite Universe.* Baltimore: The Johns Hopkins University Press. Reprinted by Harper & Row (New York, 1958).

Laity, Susan

(1987) "'The Second Burden of a Former Child': Doubling and Repetition in *A Perfect Spy.*" In *John le Carré,* edited by H. Bloom, 137–64. New York: Chelsea House Publishers.

le Carré, John

(1986) *A Perfect Spy.* New York: Knopf.

Lorenz, Konrad

(1963) *Das sogennante Böse.* Translated by M. Wilson. New York and London: Harcourt Brace Jovanovich, 1974.

(1973) *Die Rückseite des Spiegels.* Translated by R. Taylor. London: Methuen, 1977.

Lovejoy, Arthur O.
(1936) *The Great Chain of Being.* Cambridge: Harvard University Press. Reprinted by Harper & Row (New York, 1960).
Malcolm, Norman
(1960) "Anselm's Ontological Arguments." *Philosophical Review* 69:41–62.
Marcuse, Herbert
(1964) *One-Dimensional Man.* Boston: Beacon Press.
Massey, Gerald J.
(1975a) "Are There Any Good Arguments That Bad Arguments Are Bad?" *Philosophy in Context* 4:61–77.
(1975b) "In Defense of the Asymmetry." *Philosophy in Context* 4, Suppl.: 44–56.
Peirce, Charles Sanders
(1965) *Collected Papers.* Edited by C. Hartshorne and P. Weiss. Cambridge, Mass.: Belknap Press.
Philby, Kim
(1968) *My Silent War.* New York: Grove Press.
Quine, Willard Van Orman
(1948) "On What There Is." *Review of Metaphysics* 2:21–38.
Reichenbach, Hans
(1951) *The Rise of Scientific Philosophy.* Berkeley & Los Angeles: University of California Press.
Ricoeur, Paul
(1965) *De l'interprétation: essai sur Freud.* Paris: Éditions du Seuil.
Russell, Bertrand
(1918–19) "The Philosophy of Logical Atomism." Reprinted in B. Russell, *Logic and Knowledge,* edited by R. Marsh, 177–281. London: Allen & Unwin, 1956.
Scott, Dana S.
(1973) "Background to Formalization." In *Truth, Syntax, and Modality,* edited by H. Leblanc, 244–73. Amsterdam & London: North-Holland.
Singer, Dorothea Waley
(1950) *Giordano Bruno: His Life and Thought.* New York: Henry Schuman.
Southern, Richard W.
(1963) *Saint Anselm and His Biographer.* Cambridge: Cambridge University Press.
(1990) *Saint Anselm: A Portrait in a Landscape.* Cambridge: Cambridge University Press.
Strawson, P. F.
(1966) *The Bounds of Sense.* London: Methuen.

Tarski, Alfred
  (1935) "Der Wahrheitsbegriff in den formalisierten Sprachen." Translated by J. Woodger in A. Tarski, *Logic, Semantics, Metamathematics,* 152–278. Oxford: Clarendon Press, 1956.
Turing, Alan
  (1937) "On Computable Numbers, with an Application to the Entscheidungsproblem." *Proceedings of the London Mathematical Society* 42:230–65.
Wittgenstein, Ludwig
  (1958) *The Blue and Brown Books.* Edited by R. Rhees. New York: Harper & Row.

✧ Index ✧